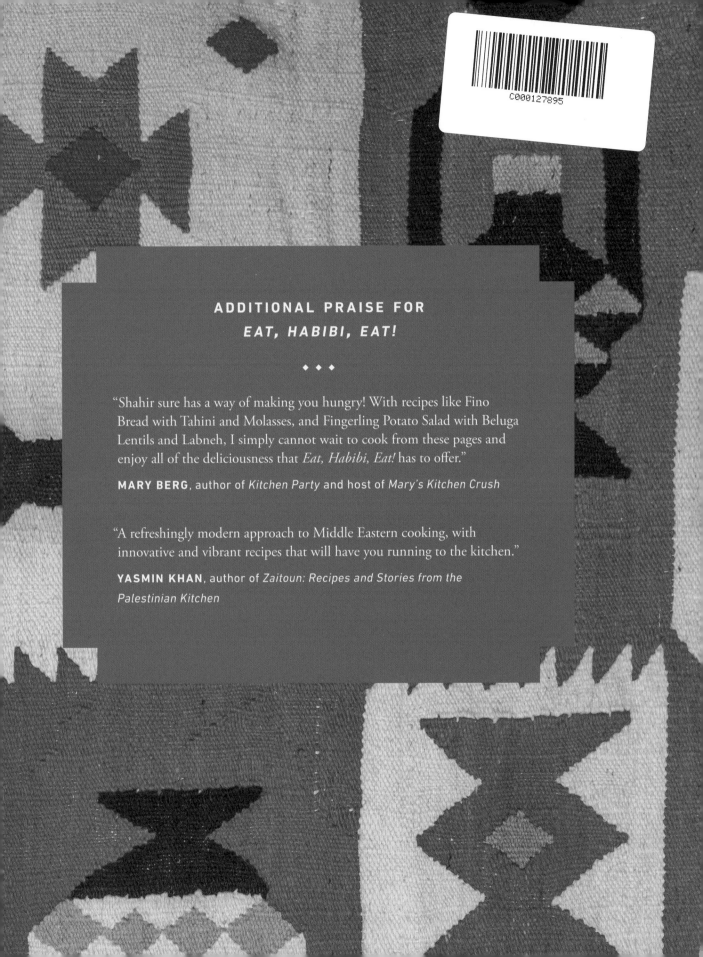

ADDITIONAL PRAISE FOR
EAT, HABIBI, EAT!

• • •

"Shahir sure has a way of making you hungry! With recipes like Fino Bread with Tahini and Molasses, and Fingerling Potato Salad with Beluga Lentils and Labneh, I simply cannot wait to cook from these pages and enjoy all of the deliciousness that *Eat, Habibi, Eat!* has to offer."

MARY BERG, author of *Kitchen Party* and host of *Mary's Kitchen Crush*

"A refreshingly modern approach to Middle Eastern cooking, with innovative and vibrant recipes that will have you running to the kitchen."

YASMIN KHAN, author of *Zaitoun: Recipes and Stories from the Palestinian Kitchen*

EAT, HABIBI, EAT!

EAT, HABIBI, EAT!

FRESH RECIPES FOR
MODERN EGYPTIAN COOKING

SHAHIR MASSOUD

appetite

Appetite by Random House™ and colophon are registered trademarks of Penguin Random House Llc.

Library and Archives of Canada Cataloguing in Publication is available upon request.

ISBN: 9780525610939
eBook ISBN: 9780525610946

Cover and book design by Emma Dolan
Photography by Kyla Zanardi

Printed and bound in China

Published in Canada by Appetite by Random House™,
a division of Penguin Random House LLC

www.penguinrandomhouse.ca

10 9 8 7 6 5 4 3 2 1

◆ ◆ ◆

This book is dedicated to my mom and dad, the two people
who told me that my decision to drop everything to go to culinary school
was reckless, ill-timed, and quite frankly . . . stupid. More importantly,
they also told me that they would love and support me anyway.

◆ ◆ ◆

CONTENTS

◆

INTRODUCTION 1

HOW TO STOCK YOUR PANTRY 9

TOOLS OF THE TRADE 16

KEY KITCHEN TIPS 18

◆

IN THE MORNING 21

APPS AND SNACKS 41

SOUPS AND SANDWICHES 73

SALADS AND SIDES 103

MAIN PLATES 137

SWEETS TO FINISH 177

ESSENTIALS 207

◆

ACKNOWLEDGMENTS 231

INDEX 234

INTRODUCTION

WHEN MY PARENTS LEFT CAIRO in 1974, in search of greater opportunities and a place to settle down and start a family, their hopes didn't include any future children becoming cooks. My mom was a pharmacist, and the goal was to find a country where she could get her professional credentials recognized so that she could practice. (This is a known, yet unexplained, phenomenon among Coptic Orthodox Egyptians: at least one in every three people must become a pharmacist. There's even a pharmacy attached to one of the churches that my parents attend. And why not? Divine intervention and prescription rash creams, all under the same roof! Total relief for whatever ails you.) My dad had an agriculture degree from Cairo University and planned to figure out what to do depending on where they ended up.

After a few short-term stops in London and New York City, where the only apartment my parents could afford was in a borderline brothel in Queens, they made their way to Montreal and, eventually, Toronto. After a few years, my mom opened her own pharmacy, where she still works to this day—over 33 years later. Dad had a less direct career path. He opened a flower shop, a printing business, worked at Radio Shack, and even started a medical equipment business before finding his calling as a real estate agent. My parents shared a strong work ethic, resiliency, and an unwavering dedication to providing for their kids. And, to their minds, the most important provision was education.

The fundamental Massoud mission never wavered: go to school, work hard, get a good job. Simple as that. However, my fascination with cooking was sparked at a young age after I learned that basic ingredients could be transformed into a finished product that people would enjoy eating. The first thing I made was a humble Rice Krispies square, compliments of the recipe on the back of the box. Inspired by the rise of culinary television, I began making late-night snacks (usually just a grilled cheese sandwich or scrambled eggs) and talking quietly under my breath as I cooked, walking my imaginary audience through the steps. Inevitably, though, I grew up and went on to graduate from a prestigious business school with a degree in accounting.

After graduation, I found a job with a large accounting firm, suckered in by the lavish recruiting parties where countless people in suits preached the gospel of public accounting as a career. They painted quite a picture, constantly proclaiming, "Accounting isn't what you think it is! It's *dynamic!*" Whether it was my naïveté or my constant intoxication from these parties, I signed on with excitement. But, as

◆ ◆ ◆

After one year, my boss was fed up and called me into his office.

"Shahir, we would like to terminate the relationship," he said matter-of-factly.

"But I didn't know we were in a relationship!" I said, squeezing in one last cheeky remark before security escorted me out.

◆ ◆ ◆

you might suspect, it didn't take me long to realize that public accounting wasn't quite the high life that the recruiters had promised. No matter how much I tried to like it, I found it mind-numbingly dull, and I started to rebel. I neglected my assignments, disrespected my superiors, and ordered singing telegrams with alarming regularity. After one year, my boss was fed up and called me into his office.

"Shahir, we would like to terminate the relationship," he said matter-of-factly.

"But I didn't know we were in a relationship!" I said, squeezing in one last cheeky remark before security escorted me out.

The same thing happened at the next firm.

During these years, the one saving grace was Sunday. Each Sunday, my roommate and I would head to a local market, grab some ingredients that looked tasty, and spend the day puttering around and cooking. Come dinnertime, we'd put on some Sinatra and sit down to our feast. Sunday was the only time that I felt some sense of control over my existence,

◆ ◆ ◆

I decided to tell the news like ripping off a Band-Aid.

"I've decided what to do next with my life. I'm going to cook."

"Like, for dinner?" my dad asked.

"No, for a living," I said.

"For a living?" My mom asked, genuinely not understanding.

◆ ◆ ◆

the only time my creative juices could flow and I could make something from what I had imagined. The meals were simple, but unknowingly, I was playing with basic and important cooking techniques: baking, roasting, steaming, marinating, etc. Each week, we tried a new ingredient, cooking tool, or presentation, and those dinners remain in my mind as some of the best meals I've ever cooked or enjoyed eating. They were the fuel for an upcoming week that was otherwise drowning in spreadsheets and work binders, and they will always be one of my few fond memories from that period in my life.

As my months of unemployment wore on but my passion for cooking continued to grow, I had an epiphany. Even though I was just five months away from qualifying as a chartered accountant, I knew I couldn't pretend anymore. I was going to cook for a living, and that was that. The only hurdle that remained was the small issue of telling my parents.

◆

ON THE AFTERNOON OF August 2, 2009, I arranged to meet my parents in downtown Toronto's historic King Edward Hotel to let them know that I had figured out what to do with my life. My poor mom was excited to see me, but my dad knew better. He figured I was either in trouble, or I needed money— or both. Nevertheless, I decided to tell the news like ripping off a Band-Aid.

"I've decided what to do next with my life. I'm going to cook."

"Like, for dinner?" my dad asked.

"No, for a living," I said.

"For a living?" My mom asked, genuinely not understanding.

When they did comprehend what I was saying, my mom immediately started sobbing, and my dad looked horrified and confused. When the server walked up to take our order, he was faced with my weeping and shell-shocked parents. To this day, my mom claims that that afternoon began a two-year continuous crying period, which I don't think is medically possible. But my mind was made up. I was moving to New York City to attend the French Culinary Institute (which is now called the Institute of Culinary Education). No amount of tears could stop me, even if it did break my heart to see my mom so upset.

◆

THE MORNING OF THE FIRST DAY of culinary school brought a new type of fear. I sat on the edge of my bed and wondered if this was a decision that was going to screw up my entire life. Would I one day look back at this moment as the turning point when everything started to go wrong? Maybe the school would give me my money back. Surely they'd understand! I could just go back home and pretend this never happened. But in that moment, I thought of my parents. I reminded myself that it was my time to hustle, just as they had. I knew I wasn't the smartest person, or the most talented, and I had little to no experience. The only ace I had up my sleeve was that I could vow to outwork everyone around me. So that's what I set out to do.

Culinary school was intensive kitchen training from day one. Within the first hour, one guy chopped the top half-inch off his finger, freaking me out even further. There was so much to learn. I nearly knocked over a woman who was carrying a giant stockpot of boiling liquid because I forgot to announce "behind." My cuts were slow and sloppy, and soon I was reaching for the bright blue Band-Aids and "finger condoms" like most of the other novices in the class. But I left that first day still determined to keep my promise to be the hardest worker in the room. The school had promised help with practical internships after the first two months, but I wanted to do more. I needed real, New York restaurant experience *right now*, so I left that first day and began looking for a job.

I had arranged to meet the chef de cuisine of Lupa after spotting an ad for line cooks on Craigslist. After school, I walked over to the quaint osteria to meet Chef Cruz Goler. He emerged from the basement, BlackBerry in hand, barely remembering our scheduled meeting. Cruz led me out the front door, and we started a street-level job interview while he glanced down at his phone. He typed away as I began spitting out my story: failed accountant, from Toronto, new to the city, looking to learn, blah, blah, blah. Cruz didn't look up. He kept fiddling with the phone, until finally I piqued his interest by saying, "Look, I know you're looking for line cooks, but I can't legally work here. What I can do is come in every day after school and do whatever you tell me to, for free." My sales pitch continued, "I just want to learn. The truth is, I don't know anything."

Cruz immediately stopped typing and looked up. "You don't know *anything*?"

"Well, basically nothing," I replied.

"You don't know how to cook an egg?"

"Not well, I don't."

Cruz thought for a moment, then countered with, "OK, but you have to come in every day after school. And show up on time. We get a lot of people who say they want to learn, and eventually they stop showing up. I don't care if it's for free. You go on the schedule. And if you don't show up, even for one shift, you're fired." Just like that, we had a deal.

We continued learning the basics of French culinary technique the following day, and after school I went to start my first shift at Lupa. At minutes before 4 pm, the dining room was eerily calm before the impending dinner storm that would follow each night. I walked through to the back, down the squeaky steps leading to the prep basement, and saw the tranquility replaced by a flurry of cooks, sous-chefs, dishwashers, and prep cooks who were feverishly getting their *mise en place* ready for the night. Cruz assigned me two simple tasks, demonstrating how he wanted them done. I was to chiffonade the Brussels sprouts and peel and cut the butternut squash.

I decided to start with the sprouts, but felt insecure about my lack of knife skills. I was slow and unsure, while everyone around me was motoring through their prep with awe-inspiring efficiency. Feeling the pressure to keep up, I started to attack the sprouts with a speed that I simply couldn't control. Slice, slice, slice, and then . . . whoosh! A blast of warmth pulsed through my thumb. My time in a professional kitchen had yet to reach the 10-minute mark, and I already had to trudge to the office for first aid. Cruz and his sous-chef, Erin, looked at the blood-soaked towel in shock. They both asked if I needed to leave for medical attention, but I refused, begging to be bandaged and gauzed up so that I could continue.

Each shift, my only task at Lupa was to prep Brussels sprouts and butternut squash. The monotony was exhausting, but the solitude was just as difficult. For the first week, nobody bothered to learn my name. I was too shy to partake in the pre-service staff meal, instead surviving on focaccia and biscotti scraps. When dinner service started, everyone scurried upstairs to the tiny kitchen, leaving me behind to tackle a seemingly giant mountain of prep. But a few guys stayed downstairs, and we eventually developed some much-needed rapport.

José was the first to break the ice. He was responsible for prepping meat, and would break down chickens and fillet whole fish with incredible ease, speed, and accuracy. His English wasn't great, but he was so kind and took the time to befriend me, making sure I ate a proper dinner with the rest of the team and teaching me the vulgar Spanish lingo I needed to survive. Together, every night, we would listen to the Spanish radio station 96.3 (*Noventa y seis punto tres! Nueva York!*) and sing along to Luis Enrique's hit "Yo No Sé Mañana," which fittingly means "I don't know tomorrow." The basement gang also featured a dedicated pasta maker named Jesús who ironically loved to talk about prostitutes in Queens, and two dishwashers, Martín and Jaime, who rounded it out. They started to call me "Shakira" instead of "Shahir," and the nickname stuck, often leading to merciless teasing whenever one of her songs came on the radio. One day when I came in to start my usual after-school shift, there were folded towels and a plain chef's jacket waiting for me, labeled with green tape: *Shakira*. I stared at the label, feeling an immense pride, then got to work.

I spent over a month on vegetable prep. One night, in a particularly glum mood, I put my peeler down and wondered what the hell I was even doing—I wasn't going to get out of the basement anytime soon; I wasn't even cooking! The temptation to leave was strong, but a seesaw dialogue in my head was trying to fight it. If I left, it would all have been a waste. I had to keep working, harder and faster. I finished the difficult shift that night and headed toward the F train to go home. Then, unexpectedly, I stopped in the middle of Houston Street and tears began to fall down my face. I was exhausted, lonely, and afraid. But I was comforted by the fact that I was working as hard as I could. I was certainly near my breaking point, but soon the perseverance would pay off.

Cruz came downstairs one night and waved at me to follow him up. Just like that, I had passed his test of commitment and he truly began to take me under his wing. First, I started in the dining room, where

the *garde-manger* station was tucked away in the corner. It was here that I would learn the gorgeous simplicity of a balanced vinaigrette dressing for escarole, cavolo nero, or misticanza salads. We would plate the contorni (beets with pistachio butter, broccoli rabe, and yes, those damn squash and sprouts), compose cold dishes (octopus with ceci, fresh tuna conserva, lengua with onion), slice meats, and put together cheese boards. The rush of preparing food for guests in a buzzing dining room was a stark contrast to the basement, and provided an unparalleled adrenaline rush.

From there Cruz moved me to the kitchen, where for the first week he told me just to watch. I stood in the corner and observed the line cooks perform with exacting precision and timing in a cramped, hot environment, working alongside each other in a finely choreographed dance. Most importantly, the food was stunning. The pasta station pumped out delicious Roman classics, while the meat station handled favorites like pollo alla diavola, saltimbocca, crispy duck agrodolce, and braised pork shoulder. Cruz and his cooks made sure that I tasted everything, exposing me to flavors and a quality that I had never experienced before. Cruz taught me how to really *taste*, to expand beyond the idea that a dish may simply be good, and understand *why* and *how* food pleased my palate. My year at Lupa, working almost every day, was so important because it was the first step in chasing my dreams, and it was the scariest leap by far. Through Cruz's referrals, I would go on to join the opening team at the Mark by Jean-Georges Vongerichten, as well as stints at Lidia Bastianich's Michelin-starred Del Posto and Keith McNally's restaurant Pulino's, a trendy spot from the famed Balthazar restaurateur.

New York City was easy to fall in love with, but when school was over and my student visa expired, it was time to go back home to Toronto. After a few years of continuous cooking and catering with wonderful chefs and restaurateurs, a start-up group hired me with hopes of growing a chain of fast-casual Italian spots all over Ontario. Building those businesses was an exhilarating ride, and I was engaged by the immense challenge that came with it, but nothing could have prepared me for the next unexpected career twist.

◆

AT THE BEGINNING OF 2016, unbeknownst to me, the CBC (the famed Canadian national broadcaster) was looking for a very specialized television host. They had green-lit a daily lifestyle show called *The Goods* that would showcase four hosts with their own areas of expertise: design, style, wellness, and food. They were having a difficult time finding the right chef host to join the cast.

Thousands of chefs from all over Canada began auditioning for the role, but I had no clue that any of this was happening. I had just finished a cooking

◆ ◆ ◆

It's safe to say that the recipes in this book are authentic to me —the kind of dishes that only a Canadian born to Egyptian parents, who was trained in French cuisine and spent the bulk of a career cooking Italian after learning in New York could make.

◆ ◆ ◆

segment on another station's morning show on behalf of the restaurant I was working at, and Portia Corman's mom was watching from her living room in Elora, Ontario. Portia was the executive producer and visionary behind the show, and her mom told her to call me, giving the world yet another example of why you should always listen to your mother. When I got the offer call, several weeks after my first audition, my journey from making those grilled cheese sandwiches as a child, to the lonely New York City basements, to the restaurant openings in Toronto all flashed before my eyes. I felt that this opportunity had been a lifetime

in the making, and my answer was an unequivocal yes—it was a childhood dream come true.

Telling my parents was one of the most joyous moments of my life, and we shared the excitement, pride, and sense of relief after all those years. It's still surreal to think that the TV station that my parents watched as new immigrants (learning the rules of hockey and keeping up with the news) would employ their son. I left my restaurant job and went on to cohost 260 episodes of daily television, meeting and cooking with my culinary heroes, including Massimo Bottura, Lidia Bastianich, Curtis Stone, and the late Anthony Bourdain. Each episode was different, and beyond the food I had the chance to interview famous musicians, authors, and movie stars; I led game show–style segments and learned about how to actually decorate my house (thanks to Steven Sabados). Every day, in front of a roaring studio audience, I had the unbelievable privilege to cook, teach, and laugh, and I never lost sight of how lucky I was to be a universe away from my old cubicle.

A few years ago, I took my now-wife Mila to New York City and we dined at Lupa for the first time. We were just beginning to date, and I wanted to show her the special place where it all began for me. It was the only occasion that I had ever sat in the dining room, finally enjoying the experience that I had watched so many others relish before, and the meal was truly spectacular. When word got out that "Shakira" was back in the building, I was treated to another wonderful surprise. José emerged from the kitchen, now as a sous-chef, beaming with pride that he personally had been cooking for us that evening. After dinner, he and I went back down to the basement and shared our respective stories of unlikely success, laughing together, almost in disbelief, before both falling silent and taking a minute to look around and appreciate just how far we had come.

And that brings us to today. It feels like a lifetime ago when I shocked my parents that afternoon in the King Edward Hotel, but despite the challenges that came with the journey—the exhaustion, self-doubt, poverty, wounds, and heartbreak—I wouldn't change a thing. That difficult decision has afforded me the privilege to cook for countless people, create menus, perform on television, and now to write my very first cookbook.

Ten years ago, I never could have predicted that the food of my childhood would become one of the biggest trends in the culinary world. When I started to cook professionally, I was fascinated by classic European techniques and dishes that were foreign to me—the idea of revisiting the staples of my youth was far removed from my consciousness. But after all the time I spent cooking foods from other cultures, I wanted to use my experiences and the lessons I'd learned to reimagine the traditions of my past, to write the kind of book that only I could.

I recreated dishes that transported me to moments centered on family, celebration, and a sense of community. I thought back to holidays when the Egyptian culinary mainstays would overflow on the table: grape leaves with yogurt and cucumber dip, kobeba, kofta, fasolia, cumin eggs, cheese squares, and enough kahk cookies to keep a kid wired for hours. Looking back, I see that I took those dishes for granted due to their ubiquity; it's not until now that I can see how special and flavorful they actually were. It seemed like every Egyptian mother put their own little spin on the roster of standard dishes, and with this book, it felt as if it was my turn to do the same.

One of the most common questions I've received throughout the making of this cookbook has been "Are these recipes *authentic*?" The answer is, of course they are, but not in the way that you might expect. For the most part, these are not the precise recipes that you would find in a traditional Middle Eastern home. This is an important disclaimer to get things started with because without such a warning, your *teta* may flip through this book and think that I'm insane—I mean, there's tarragon in the baba ghanoush!

It's safe to say that the recipes in this book are authentic to me—the kind of dishes that a Canadian born to Egyptian parents, who was trained in French cuisine and spent the bulk of his career cooking Italian food after learning in New York would make. Yes, there are bits of all of those influences in the interpretations of these modern Middle Eastern dishes, while still honoring the flavors, textures, spices, and feelings that have always come through the more traditional versions.

I hope this book inspires you to try something new, whether you're experienced in cooking Middle Eastern food, or you've never heard of sumac before. There's a liberating feeling that comes when you're cooking traditional foods in ways that are slightly different than the norm, and that feeling of playfulness and experimentation is one that can be applied to any manner of cuisines. Whatever you do, I urge you to have fun! If you think one of my recipes calls for more lemon or an extra pinch of cumin, then go for it. I've always been drawn to the kitchen because of how purely enjoyable it is, so whether you're cooking just for yourself or hosting a crowd, remember to enjoy the process. And don't forget to eat, habibi, eat!

Shahir

HOW TO STOCK YOUR PANTRY

Reading a recipe that has a laundry list of spices and ingredients can be daunting without the right pantry plan. Having an inventory of go-to ingredients will prevent that. I've compiled a list of Middle Eastern pantry staples that will make any one of these recipes accessible, broken down into key categories (assuming that you already have basics like kosher salt, black pepper, garlic powder, etc.). When shopping, I like to make a trip to the bulk food store with a list in hand, and then transfer each ingredient into labeled, resealable plastic containers to keep things fresh and organized. This way, you're always ready and confident that you can create any dish in the book without worrying about having what you need.

SPICES

When possible, try to toast and grind whole spices in small batches. The freshness and control over the texture make all the difference, especially in simple dishes where each ingredient really needs to stand out.

ALEPPO PEPPER
This could be my new go-to favorite spice, as it has less heat than chili and a little more nuance. Even though most Aleppo pepper likely comes from Turkey these days (also the source of delicious spices like pul biber and urfa biber), it is now readily available in many grocery stores. Sprinkle it on roasted veggies, add it to marinades for meat, and even use it to garnish soups to bump up the final flavor. If you can't find Aleppo pepper, you can use chili powder as a substitute.

ALLSPICE
A must in Teta Aida's Kofta (page 139), allspice deserves a spot in your earthy spice rotation. It's perfect for red meat (hence its use in a couple of the book's beef dishes) but it also plays important roles with poultry (it's a must in any jerk chicken recipe!) and even in some interesting baking.

ANISE
Generally, I use anise interchangeably with ground fennel, as they are both extremely similar and feature that gorgeous black licorice flavor. I do find it a touch milder though, and like to use it in a few desserts in the book, while pairing it with lamb as well.

BLACK SEA SALT
Specialty food stores often have countless varieties of salt. While kosher and Maldon are the most important, it is fun to have things like black sea salt in your pantry, especially when used as a finishing touch on black hummus, or on top of a fresh piece of burrata on a cheese board.

CARAWAY SEEDS
I first fell in love with caraway when my mom brought home a delicious Gouda that was studded with the whole seeds. I often pair it with fish (like Grouper Crudo with Arugula and Lemon Emulsion on page 62), add it to robust spice blends (as with Harissa on page 211), or use it to lighten up a rich pâté.

CARDAMOM

You should always buy cardamom in whole pods for the best freshness and usability. It adds light herbal notes to tea, braises, and stocks. Ground up, it is a quintessential part of any Middle Eastern spice rack.

CORIANDER SEEDS

I can't cook without fresh and toasted coriander seed. It has mild citrus notes with a warm nutty and earthy element. You'll notice that I use a ton of the stuff, often in conjunction with the next spice on this list.

CUMIN SEEDS

This book could easily have been titled *Just Add Cumin.* When in doubt, most Egyptian moms will add a little more cumin to just about anything. It's by far the most important spice in the cuisine of my youth. I highly recommend toasting and grinding the whole seed; with cumin that fresh, you need no more than salt and pepper to turn the most mundane food into something authentically Egyptian.

FENUGREEK

A staple in Indian cuisine, you can readily find whole fenugreek in the international section of most grocery stores. It provides a touch of bitterness and is absolutely required for my addictive Five-Hour "Shortcut" Basturma (page 101).

KALONJI SEEDS

This spice may require a trip to a specialty Middle Eastern store (though I did find it in my local grocery store), but it is absolutely worth it. Otherwise known as black cumin or nigella seeds, kalonji seeds have an aromatic floral and subtly bitter flavor that work as part of an interesting dukkah blend, or combined with black pepper.

LEMON, DRIED

Dried lemon combines a citrus note with a little bit of bitterness from the pith. I like that counterbalance and often find myself using it in everything from teas to marinades to complement the theme of the dish. Alternatively, look out for dried orange. You can find both at your local bulk food store.

MACE

Similarly to nutmeg, mace is a member of the spice category that should be used in moderation. It certainly belongs alongside your other earthy spices and is an integral part of my nuanced Ras el Hanout (page 215).

MAHLAB

Once you try working with mahlab, you'll never bake without it. An absolute staple in Middle Eastern cuisine, it is ground-up wild cherry pit, offering a sweet, fruity, and nutty profile to cookies and cakes. A chef friend of mine also commented that he would try it as part of a savory rub on foods to be smoked with cherry wood—not a bad idea! Look for mahlab in specialty Middle Eastern grocery stores, or buy it easily online.

MASTIC (MESTEKA)

Every classic Egyptian chicken stock must have a pinch of mastic. My local Middle Eastern grocer keeps the stuff hidden behind the cash register (I have no idea why they treat it like illicit drugs), so you may have to ask around to hunt the stuff down. Also common in old-school Greek cuisine, it is a natural resin extracted from the mastic tree, resulting in a cooling and distinctive pine/cedar flavor.

RAS EL HANOUT

This North African spice blend has a little bit of everything, and consequently has infinite uses. Make your own blend, using my recipe on page 215, or find it readily available in most grocery stores these days. Sprinkle it on your popcorn and thank me later.

SAFFRON

The world's most expensive spice, it's actually hand-picked threads from the crocus flower, hence its hefty price tag. Saffron has a beautiful bittersweet flavor and adds rich color to a dish. I also like to make compound butters and infused oils with it, which I keep on hand to improve a sauce or final plate. Don't be tempted by cheap saffron, as it's often just colored safflower strands that don't taste of anything.

SUMAC

A staple in Middle Eastern cuisine, sumac is a ground red berry that provides a tart, citrusy note. It is awesome for toasting with pita bread, topping salads, or pairing with chicken. Whenever a dish needs an acidic boost, sumac can lighten up rich flavors perfectly.

TURMERIC

Widely considered a superfood, turmeric appeals to me for the punch of color it provides (a little bit goes a long way) and the pleasant bitter property it has. Just be careful cooking with the stuff; you may dye a few wooden spoons along the way.

ZA'ATAR

Za'atar is a blend of dried herbs, sesame seeds, and spices. You can buy different versions from various countries in Middle Eastern grocers, so play around with the varieties to find your preferred blend.

HERBS

Even if I have no idea what's on the menu for the upcoming week, I make sure to grab several different herbs when shopping for groceries. I mentally divide herbs into fresh and sturdy categories. For fresh, think about herbs that are best raw—either as garnishes, as elements for salads, or as ingredients for ground meat dishes. My favorite fresh herbs to have on hand are:

- BASIL
- CHIVE
- CILANTRO
- DILL
- MINT
- PARSLEY
- TARRAGON

Sturdy herbs, on the other hand, can stand up to a long simmer in a stock, soup, or braise. Add these herbs if you have them (dare I say it, even if they're not listed in the recipe!) when hours of cooking await and you're looking to develop depth of flavor. These herbs also make wonderful infused oils that you can finish dishes with, or you can use them as a base for a salad dressing. For sturdy herbs, look for:

- ◆ ROSEMARY
- ◆ SAGE
- ◆ THYME

EGGS AND DAIRY

You certainly don't need me to remind you to pick up the butter, eggs, and milk! I always use unsalted butter so that I have control over seasoning. If you want to be a bit fancy, you can buy one pound of your everyday butter and a smaller amount of a more expensive grass-fed butter for spreading on toast. In this book, I've used large eggs for all the recipes. And as for milk, I use 2 percent for most recipes, buttermilk as a secret ingredient in my spice cake, and full-fat 35 percent cream for whipping with sugar or softening a homemade ricotta cheese.

Speaking of cheeses, try visiting your local Middle Eastern grocer to explore the world of options that are available. When I list feta cheese, for example, the varieties range from salty Egyptian or Bulgarian to balanced Iranian and crumbly Greek. Experiment with sheep's or goat's milk by asking the cheesemonger for a taste, and also figure out your desired level of firmness. The alternatives are almost endless, and that's just for the feta! Try classic Egyptian white cheese for a more mild, versatile taste or the pungent rumi cheese that's from the same family as pecorino (hence why I tend to use pecorino quite often in the book). And of course, there's halloumi, the best cheese to sear or grill.

BAKING

Baking is so fulfilling because it yields a dramatic result from the humblest ingredients. And yet, so many people have convinced themselves that they just can't do it. Whenever I meet people who emphatically state that they're not "bakers," I remind them that it's really not that hard when you measure accurately and cook at the right time and temperature.

Beyond the everyday staples needed for general baking (all-purpose flour, sugar, yeast, baking powder, etc.), there are a few new basics that you may want to grab for the book's Middle Eastern breads and desserts. First, I always have semolina flour available for my basbousa cake and fresh pasta dough. Whole wheat flour is definitely required for authentic Egyptian baladi bread, as it's responsible for the distinctive nuttiness and healthy feel.

Different thickeners play various roles in any baking kitchen as well. Cornstarch is the best for making pastry creams, tart fillings, and even dusting things like shrimp and chicken before frying. Gelatin is the necessary agent responsible for a wobbly panna cotta or creamy mishmish. And then of course there's xanthan gum—my secret for *just* thickening sauces and emulsions, while also acting as a key ingredient in homemade ice cream and gelato to avoid that annoying ice crystallization that can occur. You can find xanthan gum at most supermarkets these days, and I encourage you to give it a try—it's not as intimidating as it sounds, I promise.

Continuously buying vanilla beans is an expensive habit, while using the cheap artificial extract is less than ideal. Instead, I always have a high-quality vanilla bean paste in my fridge. It offers quality that's reasonably comparable to vanilla beans, while giving me the convenience of an extract. Find a type that you like and can afford and keep it in your rotation of baking must-haves. As for orange blossom water and rosewater, please take my advice: use with extreme caution. Do not pour these items into a recipe with reckless abandon, otherwise your food will smell like a grandmother! When used in moderation, however, they give a final product some subtle and pleasant notes.

For those "never-bakers" out there, the ingredients below will help you prepare for this book, and I'll assume you have the basics on hand. Follow the recipes as exactly as possible—you can do it!

- CHICKPEA FLOUR
- ORANGE BLOSSOM WATER
- ROSEWATER
- SEMOLINA FLOUR
- VANILLA BEAN PASTE
- WHOLE WHEAT FLOUR

NUTS, SEEDS, AND DRIED FRUITS

These ingredients play an important role in Middle Eastern fare, with countless applications in both savory and sweet dishes. With nuts, try to buy small quantities that you will use quickly. You'll also notice that I recommend toasting nuts to heighten their natural aromatic taste. Seeds are useful to have on hand to give dishes some added crunch. Feel free to interchange the dried fruits in recipes, as long as you balance the sweet and tangy chew appropriately.

- ALMONDS
- APRICOTS, DRIED
- CASHEWS
- CHERRIES, DRIED
- DATES
- MACADAMIA NUTS
- PINE NUTS
- PISTACHIO NUTS
- RAISINS
- SESAME SEEDS
- SUNFLOWER SEEDS
- UNSWEETENED COCONUT
- WALNUTS

OIL AND VINEGAR

I always have a high-smoke-point, neutral-flavored oil like canola on hand. Olive oil is great for everyday cooking, but aside from the standard Italian olive oils, be sure to try olive oil from Lebanon, Tunisia, Portugal, Spain, or Greece as well. Each region has its own unique flavor.

One of my favorite things about Middle Eastern markets is the plethora of vinegars to try. I gravitate toward pomegranate, date, and grape vinegars, but don't forget good old balsamic and even plain white vinegar as well. Trying out different oils and vinegars (with varying levels of acidity) are interesting ways to experiment and mix things up.

- ◆ BALSAMIC VINEGAR
- ◆ CANOLA OIL (OR OTHER HIGH-SMOKE-POINT, NEUTRAL-FLAVORED VEGETABLE OIL)
- ◆ DATE VINEGAR

- ◆ OLIVE OIL
- ◆ POMEGRANATE VINEGAR
- ◆ RED WINE VINEGAR
- ◆ WHITE VINEGAR
- ◆ WHITE WINE VINEGAR

MIDDLE EASTERN SPECIALTY ITEMS

All of us have a section of our pantries that's a catchall—where we store things like breadcrumbs, jam, and tomato paste. Here are the additional ingredients I have in mine.

- ◆ ASHTA (OR ARABIC DOUBLE CREAM)
- ◆ BALADI BREAD
- ◆ BLACK LIME, DRIED
- ◆ BLACK TAHINI
- ◆ CAROB MOLASSES
- ◆ FAVA BEANS, CANNED
- ◆ GRAPE LEAVES

- ◆ HIBISCUS, DRIED
- ◆ MULBERRY MOLASSES
- ◆ PICKLED TURNIPS
- ◆ POMEGRANATE MOLASSES
- ◆ SUGARCANE MOLASSES
- ◆ TAHINI
- ◆ XANTHAN GUM

A FEW NOTES ON INGREDIENTS

As you work through the recipes, there are a few key assumptions on ingredients, unless otherwise noted.

Salt refers to Diamond Crystal kosher salt, which is my go-to for everyday seasoning. It's also worth mentioning that the recipes typically feature one teaspoon of kosher salt for every pound of meat. The exception to this rule is with the tartare recipe, as colder dishes tend to need a little more seasoning.

Pepper is black and freshly ground.

Sugar is granulated white.

Fresh herbs are washed and picked, with the stems removed. I keep the stems in a freezer bag, and use them to add flavor to stock.

Eggs are large.

Milk is 2 percent.

Butter is unsalted.

Spices such as anise, caraway, cumin, and coriander should be toasted and freshly ground. The difference between having small batches of fresh spices versus the packaged pre-ground variety is like night and day. I use an electric spice grinder, but you can also go old-school with a mortar and pestle.

TOOLS OF THE TRADE

Having the right equipment and tools makes cooking easier and more enjoyable. Luckily, this doesn't necessarily mean buying everything under the sun (nobody needs a dedicated banana slicer!) or the most expensive things either. In fact, the vast majority of chefs prefer to grab items like whisks, plastic storage containers, and tongs at the local restaurant supply store for cheap, while spending money on the key pieces of equipment that will last forever, like a well-made stand mixer. Here is my list of must-haves.

CAST-IRON PAN
This is truly a necessity in any kitchen, and luckily, they are affordable these days. With uncoated cast-iron, you have to take good care of it, but it will last a lifetime if you do. I regularly use one that has an enamel coating, which is lower maintenance but still wonderful for searing steaks, making baladi bread, and even baking.

CHEF'S KNIFE
In my first month of school I lost the issued chef's knife and asked Chef Cruz what I should do, worried that I would have to buy an expensive Japanese or German brand. He told me to buy a $40 Victorinox (the same one he used), to keep it sharp, and then to buy a bag of turnips to practice my knife skills. That's exactly what I did, and I still use that very knife to this day. Your knife is your baby. It should feel perfect in your hand, making it one of those items you have to shop for in person. Try different sizes, handles, brands, etc. until you find the one that just feels right. This will likely be the knife you use the most.

DUTCH OVEN
I use a cast-iron Dutch oven for braising, stewing, making soups, etc. These retain and distribute heat and are well worth the investment required—they're one of those lifetime items.

FISH SPATULA
A fish spatula is a specialized tool with just the right amount of bend, a slight curve at the end, and well-spaced tines. It's perfect not only for flipping a delicate fillet, but also for slipping under a pan-fried latke or a seared skin-on chicken thigh, or for lifting cookies off a baking sheet.

FOOD PROCESSOR
I've had the same food processor for the past 10 years, and while the cord is mangled and the lid is beyond finicky, it still gets the job done. Make aioli, pesto, nut butters, hummus, breadcrumbs, pasta and tart dough, all with this necessary piece of equipment.

MANDOLINE
This may be debatable, but for me it's a must-have. Finely slice raw onions, shave radishes and fennel, or cut perfect potato slices for chips (make them thin enough and you can pop them into the microwave for 3 or 4 minutes for a crispy, non-fried chip . . . you're welcome).

MICROPLANE
Finely grate cheese, fresh nutmeg, chocolate, and even a cured egg yolk using this kitchen tool.

MOLDS
Silicone molds come in so many shapes and sizes—domes, squares, cubes, small ovals, and more. Use these to create stunning presentations of small cakes, set custards, and foie gras.

MINI OFFSET SPATULA
I don't find myself icing a cake every day (which is usually what you need an offset spatula for), but I reach for my mini offset spatula all the time. When

something is delicate or sticking to a baking sheet, this little tool comes in handy every time.

PARING KNIFE
Yes, only the second knife on the list so far! These little knives are the only ones for segmenting citrus, trimming delicate items, and peeling by hand. I have some serrated ones as well for slicing grape and cherry tomatoes.

PLASTIC QUART CONTAINERS AND LIDS
Otherwise known as deli containers, every single restaurant uses these for a reason. They are clear (so that you can easily see and label what's inside), sealable, reusable, stackable, and freezable. Store your spices, pantry items, and leftovers in these things to keep your kitchen world organized. And if you want the true line cook experience, crouch on the ground and eat your meal directly out of one (while guzzling water out of another one) right before your dinner guests arrive and your service starts.

ROASTING PAN
A 2½-inch-deep roasting pan is what you want for your holiday turkey (along with a wire rack), and larger quantities of braised vegetables and meats.

SERRATED KNIFE
The final knife on the list! That's right, you only really need three quality knives (unless you find yourself regularly boning out whole animals and filleting fish), and this one is great for bread, tomatoes, and generally anything delicate that could benefit from the knife's teeth to complete a cut without crushing the item.

SPICE GRINDER
As mentioned, the difference between freshly toasted and ground spices and the stale, shelf-sitting powder stuff is very noticeable. A quality spice grinder is worth the investment, as your most familiar flavors will suddenly start to taste much better. You can also grind up dried and dehydrated items into your own

delicious powders with this handy tool, allowing you to really have fun with your spice rack.

STAND MIXER
As with my food processor, I've had my stand mixer for over a decade. Use the whisk attachment for large batches of meringue or whipped cream, the paddle attachment for cookie dough, and the hook for any type of dough. It even has attachments for pasta extruding, rolling, and meat grinding. Well worth the initial investment, if you buy from a reliable brand, and it should last you for years to come.

SQUEEZE BOTTLES
Fill and label clear squeeze bottles with olive oil and canola for everyday use, infused oils for your fridge (herb or saffron are best), tahini sauce, cooking wine, and homemade mayo. Once you get into the habit, you'll never go back.

TAPE
It might sound silly, but I use green painter's tape to label everything that I cook, along with the date when it was made. It's the industry standard for attaching to the aforementioned plastic quart containers. If you're sick of reaching into your fridge or freezer and wondering "What the hell is this, and is it still good?" then get into the habit of labeling and dating. I keep my tape and a marker in the same drawer as my most used kitchen tools.

KEY KITCHEN TIPS

While there are countless tips and tricks available to help you cook better or faster, there are just a handful that I keep coming back to when I talk to home cooks. Here are my top ideas for elevating your everyday cooking.

WHEN IN DOUBT, USE ACID

I once worked with a talented, albeit eccentric, cook who approached me in the middle of service one night and screamed, "I love acid!" I think he was referring to the culinary use of lemon juice, vinegars, or the like, but with Tony you never actually knew. He was onto something, though, and the most common tip I share with home cooks is this: whenever you feel that a dish needs something, but you just can't put your finger on what it is, it's probably a hit of acidity. We often think of seasoning as simply using salt and pepper, but great cooks learn to season foods with a final hit of citrus, vinegar, or even a tangy flavor like the black lime powder and sumac showcased in this book. Acidity is the ideal counterbalance to rich, bold flavors. Almost every sauce, pesto, salad dressing, or gravy can benefit from a little hit of tang right at the end.

SEASON LIBERALLY WITH KOSHER SALT

Get in the habit of using good-quality kosher salt and seasoning your food with your fingertips. Pouring fine table salt out of a box onto your food is not seasoning—it's a game of salting roulette. Controlling each granule with your knowing hand is the skill that every great cook has to develop. This may sound funny, but practice roasting a simple vegetable with only salt, pepper, and olive oil. You may start with too much, or too little, but eventually your muscle memory and senses will find the right quantity of salt.

UNDERSTAND TIME AND TEMPERATURE

Almost all of cooking is balancing the right time and temperature. Why did my dad burn the chicken on the barbecue every summer? Simple! Too much time, on too high a temperature. Had he seared the chicken on a hot side of the grill and then transferred it to a very low side of the grill (even closing it to create an oven environment), he would have been juggling high and low temperatures and cook times like a pro. If a dish is not working out for you, take a step back and consider both of these factors. Does your oven tend to run hot? If so, consider reducing the temperature by 25°F, or baking for less time. What about your stovetop? Are you working with gas, electric coils, or induction? Each will have its own unique characteristics. Get to know your appliances, and as a great chef once told me: control your flame; don't let your flame control you!

USE YOUR SENSES

One of my chef instructors, a Frenchman named Marc Pavlovic, once told us, in his thick French accent, "I don't care what a recipe tells me, I only care about the result." That was his way of saying use your senses and think about what you're trying to achieve. For example, I talk a lot about toasting spices, and many people ask me exactly how long it will take. The most accurate answer is, it depends. How hot is your pan? How big is your pan? As I mention above, are you cooking over gas or an element? How many spices are in there? And so on, and so on. Cooking is an art, not a science. Everybody is operating with a different kitchen, environment, and idea of what constitutes "medium-high heat." In this book, I'll give you estimations on time, but please remember to think about your desired result and use all of your senses. If a recipe calls for a one-minute sear, but your steak or chicken isn't golden brown yet, then keep searing it! Smell, look, touch, and taste along the way and never lose sight of what you're trying to accomplish.

PERFECT THE BASIC TECHNIQUES

Cooking isn't rocket science. Focus on perfecting a few basic techniques that you can rely on for so many different dishes and cuisines. When you think about it, this book repeats fundamental techniques (braising, frying, poaching, searing, etc.) that you can master with the right amount of practice. Once you do, cooking anything becomes intuitive and allows for more of your own creativity.

BALANCE, BALANCE, BALANCE

Anywhere in the world, in any kind of cuisine, a common thread in great food is the idea of balance. When I taste a dish, I always look for an even balance of texture and flavor. Imagine your palate divided into sections, and make sure that each of the basic tastes isn't overpowered by any of the others. Salad dressing a bit too sweet? Throw in some bitter lettuces (endive or radicchio) to even it out. To be a great cook, you must know how to taste! The next time you are enjoying a delicious restaurant meal, take a moment to consider why it is so flavorful—exercises like this will translate when you're back in your own kitchen, juggling the culinary act of balancing flavors.

DINNER PARTY 101

Last but certainly not least, I advise you to prep for a dinner party in the same way that a well-oiled restaurant kitchen preps for a Saturday night service. That is to say, prep as much as humanly possible ahead of time—whether that means making sauces, dressings, desserts, or braised meats. Plan a menu that requires as little work as possible during the actual party, so that you can have fun hosting. For example, from this book, you could start with an easy-to-assemble salad (the Dehydrated Tomato and Parsley Tabbouleh Salad on page 131 is a visual stunner), braise the Lamb Shoulder Fattah with Orzo and Crisped Pita (page 159) the day before and reheat to serve, then finish with the Apricot Mishmish (page 194) or Brown Butter and Coconut Basbousa (page 193), both of which—you guessed it—should be made well before your guests arrive.

IN THE
MORNING

GIDO HABIB'S FUL BREAKFAST

SERVES 6
PREP TIME: 15 MINUTES
COOK TIME: 20 MINUTES

My maternal grandfather was a great man—a dedicated husband, father, and physician—who held fast to his Egyptian roots, starting with breakfast. Every morning of his adult life started with ful mudammas. These cooked fava beans are standard fuel for many Egyptians, often paired simply with bread. When I thought about tweaking this recipe to use a different bean and asked my mom for her opinion, her response was clear and emphatic. "Nooo!" she bellowed. "You can never change the fava bean in *this* recipe. The Egyptian people will never forgive you!" When your mother suggests that 100 million people will hate you, you shut up and do as you're told.

◆

BEANS

¼ cup olive oil, divided

½ red onion, finely diced

3 cloves garlic, finely minced

1 tsp + pinch salt, divided

3 tsp ground cumin

18 fl oz can fava beans, rinsed

½ cup tahini

½ cup lemon juice (about 2 lemons)

FLATBREADS

6 slices flatbread

⅓ cup olive oil

3 Tbsp butter

6 eggs

Pinch salt

1 red onion, sliced

1 tsp chili flakes

½ bunch parsley, chopped

¼ bunch cilantro, chopped

To make the beans, in a saucepan, heat 2 tablespoons of the olive oil over medium heat. Add the onion, garlic, and a pinch of salt, cooking to soften, 2 to 3 minutes. Add the cumin and the beans, along with the rest of the olive oil. Cook, breaking up the beans with a wooden spoon, for another 2 to 3 minutes.

Transfer to a bowl, then mix in the tahini, lemon juice, and ½ cup water. Season with the remaining teaspoon of salt.

To make the flatbreads, preheat the oven to 425°F. Brush each flatbread with some olive oil, then spread some of the ful mixture on each piece. Place directly on a baking sheet and bake for 7 to 9 minutes until the bread browns nicely.

Meanwhile, in a large nonstick skillet, heat the butter over medium-low heat and crack in the eggs. Fry until the whites set and the yolks are still runny. Season with a pinch of salt.

Remove the flatbreads from the oven and top with the sliced red onion. Place the eggs on top, then finish with a pinch of chili flakes and the parsley and cilantro.

◆

NOTE: You can readily find canned ful mudammas (cooked fava beans) in grocery stores these days, but if you find dried fava beans, just soak them overnight, then bring to a boil, reduce to a simmer, and cook until tender before using them in this recipe.

GLAZED ORANGE AND SPICE OLIVE OIL CAKE

SERVES 8

PREP TIME: 15 MINUTES

COOK TIME: 45 MINUTES, PLUS TIME FOR COOLING

My dad has always been a picky eater, but my mom swears that he's become even worse with age. By the looks of it, the man now survives solely on deli meat, lettuce, mustard, and cake—in no particular order. Health implications of this bizarre diet aside, I wanted to make a beautiful and moist oil-based cake that he could scarf down every morning with his coffee. Unfortunately, there will not be any deli meat or mustard-inspired recipes in the remainder of this book. Sorry, Dad.

◆

CAKE

1 cup + 1 tsp olive oil, divided

3 eggs

½ cup brown sugar

1 Tbsp vanilla bean paste, or 1 tsp vanilla extract

1 cup buttermilk

1 orange, zested, juice reserved

1½ cups all-purpose flour

2 tsp baking powder

1 tsp salt

2 tsp ground anise

1 tsp ground cardamom

¼ tsp allspice

GLAZE

1 cup powdered sugar

Orange zest, for garnish

Preheat the oven to 350°F and grease a Bundt pan with 1 teaspoon of the olive oil.

In a large mixing bowl, whisk together the eggs and brown sugar. Cream the mixture until it has increased in volume and becomes pale yellow, 3 to 4 minutes. Add the vanilla paste, the rest of the olive oil, and the buttermilk and orange zest. Whisk together.

In a separate bowl, add the flour, baking powder, salt, anise, cardamom, and allspice, and mix well. Then add the dry ingredients to the wet. Mix to incorporate, being careful not to overmix.

Pour the mixture into the greased Bundt pan and bang the pan slightly against the counter to remove any air bubbles. Bake in the oven for 40 minutes, or until a toothpick inserted into the cake comes out clean, and the cake appears to have risen and browned slightly. Remove and cool for 20 minutes, then carefully invert the pan over a rack (you can encourage the sides of the cake to release with a small paring knife if you have a bit of trouble).

Make the glaze by combining the powdered sugar with 2 tablespoons of the reserved orange juice. Pour the glaze on the cake, sprinkle some orange zest overtop, and enjoy with coffee! Serve with a side of Rosewater Whipped Cream (page 220) for a light dessert.

EGG IN A CLOUD SHAKSHUKA

SERVES 3–4
PREP TIME: 15 MINUTES
COOK TIME: 15 MINUTES

Every Easter my mom would whip up egg whites, spoon them onto bread and bake them with the yolks placed right in the middle. It was her mother, my teta's, tradition that was passed down to her, then to me, and now to you. I like to make mine as a classic shakshuka, giving the whites a head start in the oven, allowing them to get a slightly crispy and browned. By adding the yolks halfway through the cooking time, you keep them soft and bright yellow.

◆

6 eggs

3 cups Chunky Egyptian Tomato Sauce, page 223

2 Tbsp olive oil

1 tsp salt

¼ bunch parsley, finely chopped

¼ bunch dill, finely chopped

¼ bunch baby arugula

Bread, for serving

Preheat the oven to 375°F and grab a large bowl.

To separate the eggs, crack each egg in half over the bowl and shift the yolk from one half shell to the other, catching the whites in the bowl below. Once you're left with just the yolk, keep it in the half shell and place it back in the carton until the next step. Continue on with the remaining eggs.

Whip the egg whites until they form stiff peaks.

Place the tomato sauce in the bottom of an oven-safe skillet. Then, top with dollops of the whipped egg whites, creating an indentation in the center of each mound. Drizzle olive oil over each mound and add a pinch of salt. Bake without the yolks for 6 to 7 minutes, or until the whites just begin to brown and firm up.

Then remove the pan, place the yolks in each indentation and return to the oven. Bake for another 7 to 8 minutes or until the yolks have barely set and the whites are now crispy and even darker. Remove and top with the parsley, dill, and baby arugula. Serve with bread for scooping.

EGYPTIAN RICE PUDDING WITH FALL SPICES AND ORANGE

SERVES 8
PREP TIME: 40 MINUTES
COOK TIME: 45 MINUTES, PLUS
TIME FOR COOLING

Most people would consider this a dessert, but I like this creamy and not-too-sweet rice pudding for breakfast. Be careful not to overdo it with the orange blossom water, and keep the pudding on the looser end, remembering that it will firm up in the fridge. Feel free to double up on the spice blend—use the leftover spice blend to top cappuccinos, toss it with sweet potatoes for roasting, or put it in a homemade pumpkin pie.

◆

1 cup Calrose rice, well rinsed

3 cups milk

½ cup whipping cream

½ cup + 2 Tbsp sugar

1 Tbsp vanilla bean paste, or 1 tsp
  vanilla extract

¼ tsp salt

2 egg yolks

¼ tsp orange blossom water

SPICE BLEND

2 tsp cinnamon

½ tsp ground cardamom

½ tsp dried ginger

½ tsp allspice

¼ tsp grated nutmeg

GARNISH

1 cup whole almonds

4 oranges

Soak the rice in a bowl of cold water for 5 to 10 minutes, then strain. Return the strained rice to the bowl, cover with more fresh water and repeat 2 to 3 times, or until the water is no longer cloudy when the rice is sitting in it.

In a large pot, combine the soaked rice and 2 cups fresh water and bring to a boil. Reduce to a simmer and cook for 6 to 7 minutes, until the liquid has cooked off and the rice is partially cooked.

Add the milk, cream, sugar, vanilla paste, and salt to the par-cooked rice. Bring to a boil, then reduce to a low simmer and cook for 30 to 35 minutes, stirring occasionally, or until the rice is well cooked and the mixture is a tad looser than you want your final product to be.

In a small bowl, whisk the two egg yolks together. Take some of the hot rice and quickly mix it in with the yolks to temper them, then add it all back to the hot rice pudding. Stir well to incorporate and add the orange blossom water to finish. Cool slightly, then evenly spoon the rice pudding into a serving dish and refrigerate for at least 2 hours, or even overnight.

For the spice blend, while waiting for the rice pudding to set, mix the cinnamon, cardamom, ginger, allspice, and nutmeg in a small bowl.

To make the garnish, toast the almonds in a dry skillet over medium-low heat for 3 to 4 minutes, or until slightly golden and aromatic. Remove and finely chop. Suprème the oranges by running your knife down the orange to remove the skin and pith. Then, cut between the membrane walls to remove the orange segments. Cut the segments into chunks.

When the rice pudding has set in the fridge, remove and serve with a dusting of the spice blend, topped with the almonds and orange pieces.

HIBISCUS-CURED ARCTIC CHAR WITH LABNEH

SERVES 6

PREP TIME: 5 MINUTES, PLUS
30 HOURS FOR CURING

½ cup dried hibiscus

1 cup salt

1 cup sugar

1 tsp ground coriander

1 tsp ground cumin

½ tsp white pepper

½ bunch dill, finely chopped

One 12 oz arctic char fillet

1 loaf rye bread

1½ cups Labneh with Garlic Confit,
    page 217

Lemon, for zesting

½ bunch dill, for garnish

Floral dried hibiscus, otherwise known as pink sorrel, is typically reserved for use as a hot or cold tea in Middle Eastern cuisine. I happen to be more of a black coffee kind of guy, so I like to grind hibiscus into an incredible powder and use it for curing fish. In this recipe, I opt for arctic char, but you could substitute salmon or trout. Combined with tangy labneh, this is a great way to start your morning and also makes for an impressive addition to your brunch table.

◆

Grind your dried hibiscus in a spice grinder to create a vibrant pink powder.

Transfer it to a large bowl. Add the salt, sugar, coriander, cumin, white pepper, and dill to the bowl, and stir well.

Place half of the curing mixture in the bottom of a baking dish that is just large enough to house the piece of fish. Place the fish on top, then cover completely with the remaining curing mixture. Make sure to pack the mixture around the sides of the fish, and totally encapsulate the fillet in the curing solution. Let sit in your fridge for 24 to 30 hours.

Remove the fish from the curing mixture. Run the fish under cold water to completely remove all of the salt and sugar and pat dry. The fish should be firm, with a pretty pink hue to the flesh. Slice the fish thinly on the bias and serve on bread that's been slathered with labneh, with fresh lemon zest and some extra dill for garnish.

Keep the cured fish, tightly wrapped and refrigerated, for up to 3 days.

FRESH QUINCE JAM

MAKES 4 CUPS
PREP TIME: 15 MINUTES
COOK TIME: 2 HOURS
10 MINUTES

With a flavor somewhere between an apple and a pear, fresh quince is the fruit you never knew you needed. Find it in Middle Eastern grocers and cook it down into a compote or jam, use it in crumbles, or even roast it to serve with lamb chops. My mom grew up with her dad's homemade quince jam for breakfast, dolloped on top of toast with some rich and creamy ashta—aka Arabic double cream.

◆

3 quinces, peeled and cut into
    ½-inch pieces

¼ cup lemon juice (about 1 lemon)

2 cinnamon sticks

1 star anise

1 tsp dried lemon powder
    (optional, see note)

⅓ cup granulated sugar

⅔ cup brown sugar

1 Tbsp vanilla paste, or 1 tsp
    vanilla extract

½ tsp cinnamon

Pinch salt

Place the prepared quince in a large pot. Add the lemon juice and 4 cups of water. Add all remaining ingredients, then bring to a boil. Reduce the heat to medium-low and simmer gently for 2 hours. After the quince has softened and jam takes on an amber color, increase the heat to medium-high and reduce the liquid by two-thirds (this will take about 10 minutes), then cool completely. To serve, spread some cream cheese or Middle Eastern–style double cream onto your favorite toast. Spoon some quince jam on top and enjoy with tea or coffee.

Store in a resealable plastic container in your fridge for up to 10 days.

◆

NOTE: You can find dried lemon powder in your local bulk food store.

TURMERIC FAYESH

MAKES 35–40 SMALL COOKIES
PREP TIME: 20 MINUTES
COOK TIME: 50 MINUTES

Whenever someone we know goes back to Egypt for a visit, my dad asks them to bring back this crunchy morning snack to dunk in his coffee. A traditional double-baked fayesh shares a lot in common with a biscotto, but the yellow hint of turmeric sets it apart. My recipe amplifies this color by using a medium-grind cornmeal as well, giving the cookie the ideal texture for java dipping. So here you go, Dad; you no longer have to ask your friends to stuff tins of fayesh in their luggage.

◆

½ cup butter, room temperature
1 cup sugar
3 eggs, divided
½ cup milk
1½ cups all-purpose flour
1 cup medium-grind cornmeal
1½ tsp baking powder
1 tsp turmeric
1 tsp mahlab
¼ tsp salt

Preheat the oven to 350°F and line two baking sheets with parchment paper.

Cream the butter and sugar together in a stand mixer for 2 to 3 minutes or whisk them aggressively by hand for 5 to 6 minutes, until the mixture is a pale yellow and very well incorporated. Add 2 eggs, one at a time, then add the milk and whisk to mix evenly.

In a separate bowl, whisk the flour, cornmeal, baking powder, turmeric, mahlab, and salt together, then add to the butter mixture. Mix everything just until combined, being careful not to overmix.

With wet hands, divide the fayesh dough in half, and form each half into a skinny log. Place the logs on the prepared baking sheets. Whisk the remaining egg, and apply a wash to each log with a pastry brush. Bake in the preheated oven for 30 minutes.

Once the loaves of fayesh are cool enough to handle, slice individual cookies with a serrated knife, about ¼-inch thick. Lay the cookies back down on the lined sheets and return to the oven for 18 to 20 minutes, flipping halfway through. Look for the fayesh to be a very pale brown on each side—any darker and they may be too hard.

Allow to cool, then store in an airtight plastic bag or resealable container for up to 3 days.

STUFFED EGYPTIAN EGGAH WITH FETA

SERVES 4
PREP TIME: 20 MINUTES
COOK TIME: 25 MINUTES

Two omelet worlds collide in this dish, sharing the virtues that each method has to offer. Eggah is essentially an Egyptian frittata, but I wanted to start my omelet in the classic French rolled style before stuffing and baking it. Feel free to improvise with the vegetable stuffing (this is a great way to clear out your fridge for a Sunday brunch) and top with feta, Middle Eastern white cheese, or even goat cheese.

◆

VEGETABLE STUFFING

3 Tbsp olive oil, plus extra for greasing
1 zucchini, diced
1 red pepper, diced
1 yellow pepper, diced
1 white onion, diced
2 cloves garlic, minced
1 jalapeño, diced (optional)
Pinch salt
1 tsp ground cumin
1 tsp ground coriander
1 tomato, diced
¼ bunch parsley, finely chopped
½ cup crumbled feta cheese, divided

EGG MIXTURE

12 eggs
½ cup sour cream
1 tsp za'atar
½ tsp salt
½ tsp pepper
¼ tsp turmeric
¼ cup butter, divided

For the vegetable stuffing, heat the olive oil in a large skillet over medium-high heat. Add the zucchini, peppers, onion, garlic, jalapeño, and salt and cook for 2 minutes. Add the cumin and coriander and cook for an additional minute. Then add the tomato and parsley and cook for another minute or so. The vegetables should still have some bite to them. Set aside to cool slightly.

Preheat the oven to 350°F and lightly grease a baking sheet with olive oil.

To make the egg mixture, combine the eggs, sour cream, za'atar, salt, pepper, and turmeric in a bowl. Whisk well to incorporate fully.

Working in stages, heat 1 tablespoon of butter in a nonstick pan over medium-low heat. Once the butter has melted, add about 1 cup of the egg mixture to the pan.

Use a heat-resistant spatula to keep the egg mixture moving and cooking evenly. Keep moving the mixture, and create space in the pan for any uncooked liquid egg to begin to cook as well. When the mixture begins to resemble scrambled eggs, spread it around the entire bottom of the pan. Don't move the eggs for a few seconds, allowing the bottom to firm up.

At this time, fill the omelet with ¼ cup of the vegetable mixture and 2 Tbsp of feta cheese, placing each neatly in the center. Then, using your spatula, carefully flip one edge of the omelet over the stuffing, and keep rolling it over itself. The filling will be completely encased.

Remove the omelet from the pan and transfer to the baking sheet. Repeat with the rest of the egg mixture to create 4 stuffed omelets. You should have about 1 cup of vegetable mixture left over for the topping.

GARNISH

½ cup crumbled feta cheese

¼ bunch parsley

¼ bunch mint

Place the baking sheet with the omelets into the oven and bake for 9 to 10 minutes.

To garnish, remove the baking sheet and set the oven to its broil setting. Top each omelet with another ¼ cup of the reserved vegetable mixture and 2 tablespoons of feta cheese. Broil for 1 minute, until the top of the omelet and the cheese begin to brown. Remove and top with fresh parsley and mint.

FINO BREAD WITH TAHINI AND MOLASSES

MAKES 6 SMALL LOAVES

PREP TIME: 50 MINUTES, PLUS
3–4 HOURS FOR RISING

COOK TIME: 15 MINUTES

If baladi is the undisputed king of Egyptian bread, then fino is a respectable second place. Fino bread is a long, soft roll that is perfect for sandwiches, or in this case slathered with tahini and sugarcane molasses for a humble breakfast. Traditionally, it's made just as a simple Vienna roll would be, but my version benefits from a touch of yogurt to keep it moist. Make sure to warm the bread so that the tahini can melt into the fluffy center, before drizzling with molasses for some natural sweetness. Take that, peanut butter and jelly!

◆

1 cup milk

1¼ tsp active dry yeast

3 cups all-purpose flour

¼ cup sugar

1 tsp salt

3 eggs, divided

⅓ cup plain yogurt

¼ cup butter, cubed and cold, divided

Tahini, for spreading

Sugarcane molasses, for drizzling

Warm your milk in a small saucepan on the stove until it reaches 105°F to 110°F. If you're doing this without a thermometer, you should be able to place your finger in the milk and leave it for a few seconds without it being uncomfortably hot. Then sprinkle in the yeast to bloom. Let the milk and yeast sit for about 10 minutes, until the yeast is frothy. Meanwhile, whisk the flour, sugar, and salt together in a large bowl.

Transfer the milk and yeast to the bowl of a stand mixer, then add 2 of the eggs and the yogurt. Whisk gently by hand, then add the dry ingredients to the bowl. Using the dough hook attachment, mix on a low speed for 15 minutes, scraping down the sides of the bowl occasionally if necessary. Increase the speed to medium-low and mix for another 15 minutes. At this point, you can take a small piece of dough and stretch it out thinly to see if it's semi-translucent (this is a good indicator that the gluten has been developed). Increase the speed to medium-high and knead for 5 to 6 additional minutes, this time adding the cold butter in stages until incorporated. The dough may still appear to be rather wet. Crank the mixer to high speed and knead for another 5 to 7 minutes, or until the dough is coming away cleanly from the sides of the bowl. This may seem like a long process, but the development of gluten is so important with a bread dough like this.

Transfer the dough to a lightly greased bowl, and cover with a kitchen towel. Place in a warm area of your kitchen and allow to rise for 2 to 3 hours, or even overnight in your fridge, until doubled in size.

Transfer the dough to a floured work surface and divide it into 6 even pieces. If the dough feels quite wet, use some additional bench flour

to help shape it into long, skinny logs. Line 2 baking sheets with parchment paper and place 3 dough logs onto each baking sheet. Cover again loosely with a kitchen towel and proof for another 30 to 45 minutes.

Preheat the oven to 400°F. Whisk the remaining egg and paint each dough log with some egg wash.

Using kitchen shears, quickly cut 6 to 8 slits in the tops of each log and set the dough in the oven. Bake for 15 minutes or until the tops are golden brown. Allow to cool slightly before slicing. Spread tahini on the bread while it's warm, then drizzle on some good-quality sugarcane molasses.

APPS AND SNACKS

BLACK AND WHITE HUMMUS WITH SUN-DRIED TOMATO AND CARAMELIZED LEMON

SERVES 10–12

PREP TIME: 15 MINUTES, PLUS OVERNIGHT FOR SOAKING

COOK TIME: 2 HOURS

A delicious dip can have different colors, textures, and balance on your palate in the same way that a memorable entrée does. This black and white hummus achieves all of that. The "black" element comes from the special black sesame tahini and funky black garlic. The "white" is represented by white bean and a secret umami addition with the white miso. Also, don't be shy with the caramelized lemons—every bite that includes the acidic and sweet lemon is a welcome one.

♦

CARAMELIZED LEMONS

4 lemons

BLACK HUMMUS

1 cup white beans, soaked overnight

½ tsp + pinch salt, divided

⅓ cup tahini

1 Tbsp black tahini (see note)

½ cup lemon juice

1 tsp sugar

1 Tbsp white miso

3 cloves black garlic (or 1 clove plain garlic)

Ice water

TOPPING

¼ bunch parsley, leaves picked

½ cup sun-dried tomatoes, chopped

1½ Tbsp olive oil

¼ tsp black sea salt

8 mini pitas, quartered and warmed

Preheat the oven to 245°F and line a baking sheet with parchment paper.

To caramelize the lemons, trim the top and bottom off each one. Use a paring knife to remove the skin, following the contours of the fruit. Then, slice between each wall of pith to extract a segment of lemon (do this over a bowl so that you can save the lemon juice for another use, like making vinaigrette). Place the lemon segments on the prepared baking sheet and bake for 60 to 75 minutes or until they shrink up and the edges are colored. You can caramelize the lemons the day before serving, if you want to get ahead.

To make the hummus, drain the soaked white beans. In a large pot, cover the beans with water, add a generous pinch of salt, and bring to a boil. Reduce to a simmer. Cook the beans until they are very tender. This will take approximately 45 minutes, but them check periodically.

Transfer the cooked beans to a food processor and blitz with the two different tahinis, the rest of the salt, and the lemon juice, sugar, miso, and garlic. Blend until very smooth. Add some ice water, a little bit at a time, to smooth out the mixture even more. The hummus will firm up in the fridge and you want it to be easily spreadable, so add enough ice water to make it a touch looser than you want the end result to be. Blend for several minutes to make sure everything is perfectly incorporated, which will yield an aerated and light hummus.

To serve, spread the hummus on a plate, then top with the parsley, chopped sun-dried tomatoes, and caramelized lemons. Drizzle with olive oil, sprinkle with black sea salt, and serve with the warm pitas. Enjoy!

NOTE: You can find black tahini at a Middle Eastern or specialty grocery store. Use it sparingly, as it is slightly bitter. In this recipe, it's mainly added to amp up the color. If you need to omit the black tahini altogether, the hummus will still taste great but will lack the unique color. Also, never make hummus in your blender! It tends to overwork the motor, and each time I've tried it, the tired motor has needed to cool off for half an hour.

CRISPY CAULIFLOWER AND TURMERIC BITES

SERVES 6–8
PREP TIME: 15 MINUTES
COOK TIME: 20 MINUTES

Fried cauliflower is an Egyptian staple, and it's a dish I remember eating as a kid in a dimly lit tourist trap restaurant after visiting the Great Pyramids for the first time. Instead of just battering and frying the cauliflower, I combine them with breadcrumb and egg to make a neat little fritter. For the record, we were force-fed cauliflower (and broccoli for that matter) for years as children because my mom felt it was the right thing to do as a parent. I grew to love these veggies thanks to my mom, but it wasn't until years later that I realized she never ate them herself. Well played, Mom, well played.

◆

2 Tbsp + 1 tsp turmeric, divided
1 Tbsp ground cumin
Ice water
1 head cauliflower, separated into florets
2 eggs
1⅓ cups breadcrumbs
1 tsp salt
½ tsp chili powder, plus extra for garnish
Vegetable oil, for frying
¼ bunch parsley, finely chopped
¾ cup plain yogurt, for serving

◆

NOTE: These cauliflower bites are a great make-ahead recipe for entertaining. Once they've been cooked and cooled completely, freeze them in a single layer on a baking sheet. To serve, preheat the oven to 425°F and bake for 15 to 20 minutes, directly from frozen, until they are warmed through and crispy again.

Bring a large pot of salted water to a boil, along with 2 tablespoons of the turmeric and the cumin. Have a large bowl of ice water waiting so that you can stop the cooking process when you need to. Place the cauliflower florets in the boiling water for 4 minutes, then remove with a spider and immediately transfer to the ice bath.

Remove the cauliflower from the ice water and pat dry. Finely chop the cauliflower, or pulse in a food processor, to the size of a pea. You still want discernable pieces of cauliflower in your fritter, so do not chop or pulse it into a paste.

Place the chopped cauliflower in a large mixing bowl and add the eggs, breadcrumbs, salt, remaining teaspoon of turmeric, and chili powder. Mix well.

Heat 1½ inches of vegetable oil in a Dutch oven or heavy pot to 350°F and line a baking sheet with paper towel.

Using a lightly greased ice-cream scoop, grab small balls of the cauliflower fritter mixture and drop them directly into the hot oil. Be careful not to overcrowd the pot—the fritters need room to brown all over, and you don't want to drop the temperature too much. Fry the fritters for about 2 minutes, or until golden brown, then remove them with a spider. Place the fritters on the prepared baking sheet. Season with a sprinkling of salt as soon as the fritters come out of the oil, followed by the finely chopped parsley. Repeat until all of the cauliflower mixture has been fried. Serve alongside the yogurt with a pinch of chili powder on top.

MOM'S CHEESE SQUARES

SERVES 12–16

PREP TIME: 20 MINUTES, PLUS
2 HOURS FOR COOLING

COOK TIME: 30 MINUTES

My mom would make these golden cheese squares for parties and special occasions when I was young, and I would devour every last one. I have no idea how my younger self was able to consume that sheer quantity of cheese and pastry. Ah, careless youth. Anyway, cut these squares into smaller shapes for an hors d'oeuvre or go a bit larger for a light vegetarian lunch served with a tomato salad.

◆

CHEESE FILLING

3 Tbsp butter

3 Tbsp all-purpose flour

2 cups milk

¾ cup ricotta cheese

4 oz brick-style cream cheese

¼ cup blue cheese

2 Tbsp grated Grana Padano

¼ tsp white pepper

PASTRY

½ lb phyllo dough sheets (about
    12–14 sheets), thawed

1 cup butter, melted

1 egg

2 Tbsp sesame seeds

To make the cheese filling, melt the butter and flour together in a pot over medium heat. Cook for 1 minute, whisking constantly, to make a roux, then whisk in the milk. Bring the mixture to a boil, whisking constantly. Cook for 2 to 3 minutes until the mixture is thick enough to coat the back of a wooden spoon. Whisk in the ricotta, cream cheese, blue cheese, Grana Padano, and white pepper until completely incorporated, another 2 to 3 minutes.

Remove from the heat and allow to cool. Store in the fridge for at least 2 hours to cool completely, or even prepare the day before.

To make the pastry, use a pastry brush to paint some melted butter on the bottom of a baking sheet. Keep your phyllo sheets covered with a slightly damp towel to prevent them drying out as you work. Place a sheet of phyllo on the baking sheet, then brush lightly with the butter. Repeat until you've used about half of the phyllo pastry (6 sheets or so). You can trim the phyllo to fit the baking sheet exactly, or leave the overhang to create a rustic and crispy exterior.

Add the cheese filling on top and smooth out evenly with a spatula. Top the cheese layer with the other half of the phyllo sheets, again making sure to paint each layer with melted butter as you assemble. Once you're done, place the baking sheet in the fridge for 30 minutes to let the filling firm up.

Preheat the oven to 375°F. Take out the cold phyllo pastry and cheese, and cut into 24 small squares or rectangles. Using a fork, whisk up the egg with a splash of water to create your egg wash. Brush each square with egg wash and top with a sprinkle of sesame seeds. Bake for 30 minutes until golden brown and bubbling. Remove from the oven and allow to cool slightly. Enjoy warm or at room temperature.

MAHLAB FOIE GRAS WITH STRAWBERRY AND ORANGE BLOSSOM COMPOTE

SERVES 6

PREP TIME: 15 MINUTES,
PLUS OVERNIGHT FOR SETTING

COOK TIME: 5 MINUTES

I know what you must be thinking—isn't foie gras a bit of a stretch in a cookbook like this? Well, it seems the ancient Egyptians were the first to come up with the idea of fattening up geese and enjoying their rich livers. So yes, it is a stretch, but I feel like history is on my side on this one. Seasoning the foie gras with mahlab gives the dish a sweet and earthy touch, and the orange blossom in the compote provides just the right amount of floral essence. In a restaurant setting, a foie gras terrine like this is made by using several lobes and filling an entire loaf pan. But for the home cook, I've created this method that allows you to use a minimal amount of foie gras while still serving it up in style with the help of a trusty silicone mold.

◆

FOIE GRAS

⅓ lb foie gras, cleaned and
  deveined

½ tsp mahlab

Pinch white pepper

Pinch salt

Splash brandy (optional)

**STRAWBERRY AND ORANGE
BLOSSOM COMPOTE**

2 Tbsp sugar

½ lb strawberries, finely diced

½ tsp black pepper

¼ tsp orange blossom water

4-inch silicone mold (see p. 16)

Crispy bread, for serving

To make the foie gras, cut the foie gras into slices and place in a small baking dish. Cover with the mahlab, pepper, salt, and brandy. Place a piece of plastic wrap directly on the surface of the foie gras and refrigerate for at least 4 hours to allow the flavors to penetrate.

Meanwhile, make the compote. In a small saucepan, bring 2 tablespoons of water and the sugar to a gentle boil, then add the strawberries. Cook briefly for 1 to 2 minutes, so that there's still some structure to the strawberries. Remove from the heat and cool. Add the black pepper and the orange blossom water.

Once the foie gras has marinated, remove it from the fridge and fill a bowl with ice.

Place the foie gras in a heatproof bowl and set over a pot of simmering water. Move the foie gras around until it begins to melt and reaches a temperature of about 125°F. It should feel warm to the touch, but not hot enough to make your finger uncomfortable. When the foie gras reaches temperature, remove the bowl from the double boiler and place over the bowl of ice. Move the melted foie gras around with a spatula until it begins to thicken slightly and emulsify again. You will notice the foie gras coming back together and becoming homogeneous and lighter in color.

Transfer the cooled foie gras to your mold and chill completely in the fridge for at least 6 hours, but preferably overnight. After the foie gras has chilled, remove it from the mold, let it come to room temperature, and serve on a plate with the compote and some crispy bread.

PINK AND GOLD BEET DIP WITH PINE NUTS

SERVES 8
PREP TIME: 15 MINUTES
COOK TIME: 2 HOURS

A bright pink dip made of pureed beets has always been one of my favorite dishes, both aesthetically and in terms of taste. But mixing a sunshine-yellow beet dip into the equation takes this classic to uncharted, borderline tie-dyed levels of presentation that people will love. It's an extra step to make two different batches of dip, but when you bring them together and combine them with all those finishing touches, it's a real showstopper.

◆

3 medium-sized red beets

3 medium-sized yellow beets

½ tsp turmeric

4 cloves garlic, divided

1 cup Greek yogurt, divided

1 cup tahini, divided

2 tsp salt, divided

2 tsp ground cumin, divided

2 tsp ground coriander, divided

2 Tbsp lemon juice, divided

GARNISH

⅓ cup pine nuts, toasted and chopped

¼ bunch chives, finely chopped

1 Tbsp za'atar

2 Tbsp olive oil

Preheat the oven to 400°F. Wrap the red beets in a tight foil packet, and wrap the yellow beets in a separate foil packet. Try to find beets of similar size so that they cook in the same amount of time, and keep the yellow beets separate from the red ones to preserve their contrasting color.

Roast on a baking sheet for 1½ to 2 hours, or until very tender. Remove the beets from the oven, unwrap them from the foil packets, and peel while still warm. Chop the peeled beets, reserving ½ cup of the yellow beets for garnish.

Puree the yellow beet dip first. Place the peeled and chopped yellow beets in the food processor and add the turmeric. Then add 2 cloves of garlic, ½ cup of the yogurt, ½ cup of the tahini, 1 teaspoon each of salt, cumin, and coriander, and 1 tablespoon of lemon juice. Puree until very smooth. Remove from the food processor and transfer to a bowl.

Repeat with the red beets. Add them to the food processor along with the remaining garlic, yogurt, tahini, salt, cumin, coriander, and lemon juice. Blend until very smooth.

To plate, place a dollop of the yellow beet dip on the bottom of your serving bowl. Top with some of the red beet dip, then artfully draw swirls through the whole thing with an offset spatula or the tip of a knife. Creatively add more dollops of the contrasting colors to create a unique look. To finish, top with the pine nuts, chives, za'atar, olive oil, and the leftover yellow beets. Most importantly, post a picture of all this hard work on Instagram before you dig in!

CHICKPEA FRIES WITH HARISSA MAYO

SERVES 8

PREP TIME: 15 MINUTES, PLUS 4 HOURS FOR COOLING

COOK TIME: 25 MINUTES

I developed this recipe for a TV segment a few years back and have been hooked ever since. Chickpea flour is just ground chickpeas and can be found in bulk food stores and in most regular grocery stores these days. Once you master the basic technique of cooking the seasoned chickpea flour until it thickens and cools, you can get creative with different flavors and shapes. These fries are best when served right away.

◆

4 cups beef or vegetable stock

2 cups chickpea flour

1 tsp salt

1 Tbsp ground coriander

1 tsp garlic powder

1 tsp onion powder

1 Tbsp butter

Vegetable oil for frying

HARISSA MAYO

½ cup Garlic Mayo, page 209

½ cup ketchup

2 Tbsp Harissa, page 211

Pinch salt

Paprika, for garnish

¼ bunch chives, finely sliced, for garnish

Bring the stock to a boil in a large pot over medium-high heat and line a baking sheet with parchment paper.

Mix the chickpea flour, salt, coriander, garlic powder, and onion powder together in a bowl. Slowly add the seasoned chickpea flour to the boiling stock, whisking constantly to prevent any lumps forming. While whisking, reduce the heat to medium-low. Whisking regularly, cook for 10 to 12 minutes, or until the mixture pulls away from the sides of the pot and is quite thick (this is important so that the fries don't fall apart in the oil). Remove the mixture from the heat, then whisk in the butter to finish.

Pour the mixture into the lined baking sheet and spread evenly with an offset spatula. Place a second piece of parchment directly on top, then place another baking sheet on top to perfectly flatten the mixture (optional, but leads to perfectly shaped fries). Refrigerate for at least 4 hours or even overnight to firm up.

Make the harissa mayo by mixing the garlic mayo, ketchup, harissa, and salt to taste. Set aside.

Once the chickpea flour mixture has firmed up, remove it from the baking sheet and invert onto a cutting board. Cut the solid mixture into evenly shaped fries—this recipe should yield about 40 in total.

Heat your vegetable oil to 350°F in a Dutch oven or heavy-bottomed pot and line a baking sheet with paper towel. Slowly add the fries to the hot oil, working in stages (8 to 10 fries at a time). Fry for 1 to 2 minutes, or until the exterior is golden brown. Remove the fries to the baking sheet and season with a few pinches of salt. Repeat until all of the fries have been cooked. Sprinkle a pinch of paprika and the chives on the mayo and serve alongside the fries.

MANGO-GLAZED OLIVES AND SUN-DRIED TOMATOES

MAKES 2 CUPS
PREP TIME: 5 MINUTES
COOK TIME: 10 MINUTES

This could be the easiest recipe in the entire book, but it's one that has a place at the beginning of every party you host. Reduced mango juice coats briny Moroccan and Lebanese olives with complementary sweetness, while the chili flakes give each bite some zing. Serve as part of your meat and cheese board, and you might even experiment with other juices from time to time.

◆

¾ cup Moroccan black olives

¾ cup Lebanese green olives

½ cup sun-dried tomatoes, julienned

1½ cups mango juice

¼ tsp chili flakes

2 Tbsp finely chopped parsley

Combine the olives, sun-dried tomatoes, mango juice, and chili flakes in a pot and bring to a boil over high heat. Reduce the heat to medium-high and cook until all the liquid has evaporated and the olives are evenly coated in the glaze, about 10 minutes. Finish by stirring in the fresh parsley and serve warm or at room temperature.

WHIPPED FETA WITH EGGPLANT RELISH

SERVES 6—8

PREP TIME: 30 MINUTES, PLUS TIME FOR COOLING

COOK TIME: 30 MINUTES

While hard, crumbly feta gets most of the attention, there are softer varieties that can be transformed into a velvety whipped dip. I like to use an Egyptian version that's not too salty, but you can use any type of softer, milder feta that's available. The eggplant relish brings the dish some needed acidity and can be used as a condiment for other dips, vegetables, and meats.

◆

EGGPLANT RELISH

1 Tbsp coriander seeds

1 Tbsp cumin seeds

1 tsp mustard seeds

4 cardamom pods

2 Roma tomatoes, peeled and diced

1 cup olive oil

1 eggplant, diced

1 red onion, finely diced

5 cloves garlic, minced

1 carrot, finely diced

3 green chilies, finely minced

3 Tbsp sugar

1½ tsp salt

¼ cup + 2 Tbsp white vinegar

½ bunch mint, finely chopped

¼ bunch parsley, finely chopped

WHIPPED FETA

7 oz soft feta cheese, about 2 cups (see note)

1 cup whipping cream

Start by making your eggplant relish. In a dry frying pan over medium-low heat, toast the coriander, cumin, and mustard seeds and the cardamom pods for 3 to 4 minutes, until fragrant.

Grind the spices using a spice grinder or mortar and pestle and set aside.

Bring a pot of water to a boil over high heat and prepare a bowl of ice water. Cut an "X" into the top of each Roma tomato, then plunge the tomatoes into the boiling water. Blanch for 1 minute, then remove and place in the bowl of ice water. Once slightly chilled, remove the tomatoes and peel away the skins, starting from the X. Dice the tomatoes.

Line a baking sheet with paper towel. In a large skillet, heat the oil over medium-high heat. Add the eggplant and reduce the heat to medium. Cook for 7 to 8 minutes, until the eggplant is golden brown and has soaked up a bit of the oil. Use a slotted spoon to transfer the eggplant to the prepared baking sheet.

Remove the pan from the heat, allowing it to cool slightly, then add the onion, garlic, carrot, and chilies. Return to the heat and cook on medium-low for 4 to 5 minutes, or until the onion is softened and semi-translucent. Add the ground spices and cook for another minute. Add the sugar and tomatoes, cooking for an additional 1 to 2 minutes. Return the eggplant to the pan, along with the salt, vinegar, mint and parsley. Mix well, then allow to cool completely before storing in a resealable plastic container for up to 1 week in your fridge.

For the whipped feta, bring the feta to room temperature, then combine with the whipping cream in a large mixing bowl. Use an electric mixer to whip air into the feta and cream. Keep whipping until the feta

NOTE: If you can't find a soft feta, feel free to substitute goat cheese. You'll end up with the same smooth consistency and similar flavor.

reaches a medium-hard peak (remember that it will firm up in the fridge). Taste for seasoning and adjust if necessary. Cover the bowl with plastic wrap, then transfer the whipped feta to the fridge for an hour or two to allow it to firm up slightly.

To serve, smear the whipped feta on a plate, swirl it in a bowl, or you can even pipe it elegantly if you feel like being fancy. Serve alongside the eggplant relish with some good bread.

SWEET AND SPICED NUT MEDLEY

MAKES 2 CUPS
PREP TIME: 10 MINUTES
COOK TIME: 10 MINUTES

When I was growing up, every family party started with the adults sipping drinks and cracking open pistachio shells before shoveling them into their mouths while managing to talk animatedly at the same time. These days, you can buy any number of nuts already toasted and salted, but I prefer to come up with my own sweet and savory seasoning. The egg whites are the best glue to hold the spices on the nuts. I've put together some balanced flavors to match the medley of nuts, but don't let this recipe constrain you—experiment with your own mix until you land on your ideal balance of sweet spice.

◆

1 egg white
2 Tbsp brown sugar
1 tsp smoked paprika
½ tsp Ras el Hanout, page 215
½ tsp ground coriander
½ tsp dried orange (optional)
¼ tsp chili flakes
¼ tsp dried mint
¼ tsp dried parsley
½ tsp salt
¾ cup whole blanched almonds
¾ cup shelled pistachios
¼ cup pine nuts
2 Tbsp sesame seeds

Preheat the oven to 400°F and line a baking sheet with parchment paper.

In a large bowl, whisk the egg white until a firm peak is formed. Then, mix in the sugar, spices, and herbs evenly. Using a spatula, fold the nuts and sesame seeds into the egg white mixture, then spread in an even layer on the baking sheet. Bake for 9 to 10 minutes until golden and toasted. Allow to cool slightly before breaking up any stuck-together nuts. Store in a resealable plastic container for up to 1 week.

CHICKEN LIVER MOUSSE WITH DATE VINEGAR GLAZE

SERVES 8–10

PREP TIME: 15 MINUTES, PLUS 4 HOURS FOR SOAKING AND SETTING

COOK TIME: 20 MINUTES

I have an important relationship with this recipe! It sounds like a bad country song, but I once got dumped and left with no girl, no apartment, and no job prospects. Things were bleak, but a glimmer of hope presented itself when I won a local chicken liver pâté contest with this recipe, beating some of the top chefs in the city. Shortly after, my dad called me and wisely said that I might not have much going for me now, but at least I was the pâté champion of Toronto! What a guy.

◆

CHICKEN LIVER MOUSSE

1 lb chicken livers

1 cup milk

3 Tbsp olive oil

1 white onion, minced

5 cloves garlic, minced

½ bunch thyme sprigs, stems attached

1 tsp caraway seeds

Pinch salt

¼ cup brandy

¼ cup sour cream

2 Tbsp lemon juice

4 Tbsp cold butter, cubed

½ bunch parsley, chopped

DATE VINEGAR GLAZE

½ tsp powdered gelatin

⅓ cup date or balsamic vinegar

2 Tbsp sugar

GARNISH

Parsley leaves

Mint leaves

Dill, freshly picked

Black pepper

To make the mousse, clean your chicken livers and trim them of any excess fat, then soak in the milk for 2 to 4 hours. This mellows out the flavor of the liver. Once the livers have soaked in the milk, remove and pat dry with a paper towel. Discard the milk.

In a large skillet, heat the oil on medium-low and sweat the onion, garlic, thyme, and caraway seeds with a pinch of salt. Cook for 8 to 10 minutes until soft and translucent, stirring often. Add the livers and increase the heat to medium-high, adding a little oil if needed. Cook for approximately 3 minutes, or until the livers have just a trace of pink on the inside. Add the brandy and cook for another minute to reduce.

Remove from the heat, pull out the thyme stems, and transfer the liver mixture to a food processor. Add the sour cream and lemon juice, then blitz for 1 to 2 minutes, or until the liver is nicely whipped and ultra-smooth. Leave the processor running and drop in the cubes of butter. Blend for another minute or so until the butter is incorporated. Turn off the food processor and scrape down the sides of the bowl. Add the parsley and blitz for another minute. Taste for seasoning and add a pinch of salt if required.

Make your date vinegar glaze next. Place 1 tablespoon of hot water in a small bowl and add the gelatin. Bring the vinegar and sugar to a gentle boil in a small skillet over medium-high heat. Pour in the bloomed gelatin and swirl to incorporate. Reduce to a simmer for 1 to 2 minutes, then transfer to a new bowl to cool.

Pour the chicken liver mousse into a serving dish. Small ramekins work well, or you can use a larger, shallower dish for entertaining a crowd. Smooth out the mousse with an offset spatula, then place the garnishing herbs on top. When the glaze has cooled slightly, pour it overtop of the mousse and herbs. Set in the fridge for at least 4 hours or overnight to firm up. Serve at room temperature, topped with freshly cracked black pepper and fresh bread on the side.

GROUPER CRUDO WITH ARUGULA AND LEMON EMULSION

SERVES 2–3
PREP TIME: 25 MINUTES

The last time I saw my Uncle Maher was on his boat in Hurghada with my dad and a few of their friends. I spent the morning snorkeling, soaking up the sun, and drinking Egyptian beers—all while my uncle tried to catch us a fish for lunch. After a few unsuccessful hours, he finally yelled out in excitement. We all turned around to see Maher proudly showing off his bounty. Within a few minutes the fish (everyone claimed it was grouper) was cleaned and barely cooked, garnished only with fresh lemon. He served it with a simple arugula salad (otherwise known as *gargeer*), some tahini, and more beers. This crudo embodies the freshness and simplicity of such a perfect dish, on such a perfect day.

◆

ARUGULA AND LEMON EMULSION
2 cups arugula
1 Tbsp lemon juice
⅛ tsp xanthan gum (see note)
Pinch salt

TAHINI MUSTARD
¼ cup tahini
¼ cup Garlic Mayo, page 209
1 Tbsp Dijon mustard
1 Tbsp lemon juice
Pinch salt

GROUPER CRUDO
6 oz grouper or sea bream fillet

GARNISH
2 radishes, finely sliced
Zest of 1 lemon
2 Tbsp olive oil
1 tsp caraway seeds, toasted and ground (or substitute with ground caraway)
¼ tsp Maldon salt

Make the arugula and lemon emulsion by combining the arugula, lemon juice, salt, and ½ cup water in a blender. Turn to the lowest setting, then slowly add the xanthan gum. Blend for 30 seconds to combine, then transfer to a separate bowl.

For the tahini mustard, combine the tahini, garlic mayo, mustard, and lemon juice in a bowl. Add 2 to 3 tablespoons of water to loosen the mixture, along with a pinch of salt. Whisk well to incorporate, then transfer to a resealable plastic container or squeeze bottle. Refrigerate until ready to use.

To make the crudo, carefully slice the fish using a very sharp knife. Hold your knife at a 45-degree angle to the fish to create clean cuts and avoid tearing the flesh.

Place some of the arugula and lemon emulsion on the bottom of a serving plate. Delicately place the fish evenly overtop. Top with the radishes, lemon zest, a drizzle of olive oil, and a sprinkle of the ground caraway. Dollop a bit of the tahini mustard on each piece of fish, then finish with a pinch of Maldon salt.

◆

NOTE: Xanthan gum sounds intimidating, but it's extremely easy to use. It's perfect for just slightly thickening dressings, emulsions, and sauces and is becoming widely available in grocery stores.

MOM'S HOLIDAY CUMIN EGGS

SERVES 8–10
PREP TIME: 20 MINUTES
COOK TIME: 10 MINUTES

Every Christmas my mom would make these simple, tasty hard-boiled eggs coated in butter and cumin. The smell of cumin toasting in that butter would call me into the kitchen, and even as a kid I could devour egg after egg. Which reminds me of a life lesson: don't eat more than five eggs in one sitting and expect to feel remotely OK. Anyway, I've made a deviled-egg version of this dish that gives the same crispy cumin flavor profile, but in a more entertaining-friendly way. It's the perfect finger food for a holiday party.

◆

8 eggs
½ tsp salt
½ cup Garlic Mayo, page 209
2 Tbsp ground cumin
1½ Tbsp butter
8 sprigs dill
2 tsp Maldon salt

Bring a saucepan of water to a boil over high heat and prepare an ice bath. Place the eggs in the boiling water for exactly 9 minutes, then immediately transfer to the ice bath. Cool, then peel the eggs, and slice them in half lengthwise.

Place the yolks in a bowl with the salt and garlic mayo and combine well.

Take the hollowed egg whites and place them cut side down on a plate with the ground cumin, shaking off any excess.

Melt the butter in a frying pan set over medium heat and add the egg whites, cut side down, to toast the cumin. Toast until the cumin is a deep golden brown, and don't worry if parts of the egg whites start to puff and caramelize.

Allow to cool slightly, then refill with the yolk and mayo mixture. Top with a sprig of dill and sprinkling of coarse Maldon salt.

CRISPY GRAPE LEAVES WITH BRAISED LAMB AND SPICED RICE

SERVES 16–18

PREP TIME: 1 HOUR, PLUS 4 HOURS FOR MARINATING

COOK TIME: 4 HOURS

I always loved the flavors of classic stuffed grape leaves but longed for some texture. The rice, meat, and leaves tasted amazing, but together were all so soft. Here, I've reimagined the dish, while still bringing in all the tastes that make it nostalgic for me. This recipe may seem complicated, but the rice, meat, and grape leaf powder can all be made well in advance, and it freezes well too. If you're short on time, you can skip the breading and frying and serve this as a main course as rice topped with the lamb, yogurt, and flavor-packed grape leaf dust.

◆

The first step is to coat the lamb in the cinnamon, paprika, onion powder, garlic powder, cumin, coriander, aniseed, and chili flakes. Marinate in the fridge for at least 4 hours, up to overnight, to allow the flavors to permeate the meat. Once the lamb is ready, preheat the oven to 350°F.

LAMB

2.5–3 lb bone-in leg of lamb

2 tsp cinnamon

1 Tbsp smoked paprika

1 Tbsp onion powder

1 tsp garlic powder

1 tsp cumin seeds, toasted then ground

1 tsp coriander seeds, toasted then ground

1 tsp aniseed, toasted then ground

¼ tsp chili flakes

2 white onions, roughly chopped

3 cloves garlic, smashed

1 tsp salt

2 cups beef stock

3 bay leaves

Place the onions and garlic in the bottom of a roasting pan, then place the lamb on top and season with salt. Add the stock and bay leaves, then cover with foil. Slowly braise in the oven for 3 to 3½ hours, until the meat is fall-apart tender. Shred the meat and combine with the jus and softened onions and garlic. This method is foolproof and can be done a day or two in advance.

To make the grape leaf powder, preheat the oven to 225°F or the lowest possible temperature setting. Spread the grape leaves out on a baking sheet and dehydrate in the oven for 1 to 1½ hours, until hardened. Place the dried grape leaves in the spice grinder and turn into a powder. This powder is good for up to 1 week.

GRAPE LEAF POWDER

32 grape leaves

To make the rice, place a large pot over low heat. Heat 3 tablespoons of the olive oil, then add the onions, garlic, and a pinch of salt. Cook until soft, about 10 minutes. Add the rice and toast for 1 minute, adding an additional tablespoon of olive oil if necessary. Add the ground cumin, coriander, fennel, and caraway to toast as well. Gradually add the stock and a generous pinch of salt and cook for about 20 minutes, stirring regularly. Taste for seasoning and add salt if needed. Add the butter for a glossy finish, and transfer the rice to a baking sheet to halt the cooking process. Allow the rice to cool completely before the next step.

RICE

4 Tbsp olive oil, divided

1 white onion, finely minced

3 cloves garlic, finely minced

Salt

1 cup Arborio rice

1 Tbsp cumin seeds, toasted then ground

1 Tbsp coriander seeds, toasted then ground

1 Tbsp fennel seeds, toasted then ground

1 Tbsp caraway seeds, toasted then ground

6 cups beef stock

1 Tbsp butter

BREADING AND FRYING

Vegetable oil, for frying

2 cups all-purpose flour

4 eggs, scrambled

3 cups panko breadcrumbs

TO SERVE

1 cup Cucumber and Garlic Yogurt, page 210

To fry the rice balls, heat the vegetable oil in a Dutch oven or heavy bottomed pot to 350°F and line a baking sheet with paper towel. Form a ball of cooled rice about the size of a golf ball (a scant ¼ cup's worth). Make an indent, then stuff it with some of the cooled lamb meat. Close the ball then roll it back into a circle. Repeat until all the rice has been used.

Set up the breading station with a separate bowl each for the flour, egg, and breadcrumbs. Dip each rice ball in flour, then egg, then bread-crumbs and fry in the oil for 3 to 4 minutes, until golden brown. Work in batches so that the temperature of the oil doesn't drop. Remove the rice balls from the oil, transfer to the prepared baking sheet, and add a pinch of salt while the balls are still warm.

Serve with the yogurt, and top with grape leaf powder.

◆

NOTE: The spices for the rice may seem like a lot, but they provide a hearty and full flavor. Also, you'll likely have leftover braised lamb, even after stuffing all of the rice balls. The lamb freezes very well in a resealable plastic container; just make sure to cover the meat in some of the braising liquid.

MIDDLE EASTERN STEAK TARTARE WITH LEMON SABAYON

SERVES 6
PREP TIME: 30 MINUTES
COOK TIME: 30 MINUTES

I remember watching a *Mr. Bean* episode where the title character wanders into a fancy restaurant and mistakenly orders steak tartare. At 10 years old, I cringed in horror—who would eat raw meat? While my parents still probably feel this way, I grew to love this dish as an adult, and kept versions on my menus throughout the years. Use the freshest beef you can find and try this sabayon technique instead of the standard egg yolk on top.

◆

TARTARE
1 lb beef tenderloin or top sirloin
2 Tbsp minced shallot
2 Tbsp minced pickled turnips
2 Tbsp finely chopped parsley
2 Tbsp finely chopped mint
2 Tbsp finely chopped cilantro
1½ tsp salt
2 Tbsp Harissa, page 211
2 Tbsp Garlic Mayo, page 209
Crispy bread, for serving

LEMON SABAYON
2 Tbsp lemon juice
2 egg yolks
1 tsp hot sauce

To make the tartare, first make sure that the meat is cold and your knife is sharp. Finely mince the meat and place in a bowl. I prefer to do this by hand rather than using a food processor or meat grinder. Add the shallot, turnip, parsley, mint, cilantro, salt, harissa, and garlic mayo and mix well. Place in a plastic container or nonreactive bowl, cover, and refrigerate until ready to serve.

For the sabayon, place a pot of water over medium-low heat and bring to a gentle simmer.

In a heat-resistant bowl, combine the lemon juice and egg yolks. Place the bowl over the pot of simmering water and whisk well for 5 minutes, taking care to scrape down the sides and keep the mixture aerated. Whisk until the sabayon doubles in size and until you can lift the whisk and draw a figure eight with the mixture, about 20 minutes. Stir in the hot sauce, and allow to cool.

To plate the final dish, begin by drizzling some of the sabayon on the bottom of the plate. Then, take a ring mold and place about 1 cup of tartare in the middle. Spread out the meat with a spoon to fit the shape of the mold and serve with a side of crispy bread.

TARRAGON BABA GHANOUSH

SERVES 6–8
PREP TIME: 20 MINUTES, PLUS
20 MINUTES FOR STRAINING
COOK TIME: 25 MINUTES

Charring eggplant over an open flame is an almost mandatory step in getting that smoky flavor that one expects from a solid baba ghanoush. As for the tarragon, it's truly the most underrated herb, and I thought that its delicate touch and gentle anise flavor would work nicely with the robust smokiness of the eggplant. This version combines some favorite French elements with the spirit of a creamy Israeli baba ghanoush so well that you'll never look at eggplant dip the same way.

◆

1 medium-sized eggplant

⅓ cup crème fraîche or full-fat sour cream

¼ cup mayonnaise

1 Tbsp tahini

1 clove garlic, minced

2 Tbsp lemon juice

1 Tbsp olive oil

¾ tsp salt

½ bunch tarragon, finely chopped

Poke your eggplant with a sharp knife in several spots and place a piece of aluminum foil underneath a gas element. Roast the eggplant directly over a medium-low flame for 20 to 25 minutes, rearranging it from time to time carefully with tongs. The juices from the eggplant will release and drip onto your stovetop, so the layer of foil underneath the burner is helpful for cleanup.

Remove the eggplant from the flame, and cut it in half lengthwise on a cutting board. Scoop out the softened flesh with a spoon and place it in a strainer sitting on top of a bowl to allow the excess liquid to drain. Take the time to remove any blackened bits of skin, as they are quite bitter at this point. Leave the eggplant to strain for 20 minutes, occasionally pressing down on the flesh with the back of a spoon to speed up the process.

Combine the crème fraîche, mayonnaise, tahini, garlic, lemon juice, olive oil, and salt into a large mixing bowl. Whisk well. When the eggplant has completely drained, add the roasted flesh to the bowl and mix. Add the fresh tarragon.

Transfer to a bowl or a plastic container to be kept in the fridge for up to 3 days. Serve with crusty bread and a generous glug of olive oil on top.

◆

NOTE: If you don't have a gas burner at home, you can peel and cube the eggplant then roast (or even broil) the flesh in a 450°F oven until it's tender and blistered on the outside. You won't get the same smoky flavor, so I would garnish it with a pinch of smoked sea salt to try to mimic the taste. It should also be noted that tarragon is criminally underrated—use it with any fish or poultry recipes.

SOUPS AND SANDWICHES

SPINACH AND KALE MULUKHIYAH WITH CRISPED AND SPICED RABBIT

SERVES 6 TO 8
PREP TIME: 20 MINUTES
COOK TIME: 1 HOUR 20 MINUTES

This is one of those dishes that some Egyptian people obsess over. My dad has an eccentric, albeit predictable, friend named Naguib who will eat this soup daily. Typically, it's made with jute leaves, called *mulukhiyah*—a unique Middle Eastern ingredient you can find in specialty grocers. But I've swapped this out for frozen spinach and kale because the flavor profile is similar, and just as good. Try it with the rabbit or use chicken instead.

◆

2 lb rabbit legs or chicken legs
6 cups chicken stock
3 bay leaves
2 cinnamon sticks
3 cloves garlic, smashed
6 cardamom pods
1 tsp allspice
1 Tbsp coriander seeds

SPICE MIX
¼ tsp cinnamon
¼ tsp allspice
¼ tsp black pepper

SOUP
2 Tbsp olive oil
1 onion, minced
3 cloves garlic, minced
One 10 oz container frozen
  spinach
2 cups frozen kale
1 tsp salt

BROWN BUTTER
¼ cup butter
2 cloves garlic, minced
1 tsp ground coriander
3 cups Egyptian Rice, page 212

In a large pot, place the rabbit, stock, bay leaves, cinnamon sticks, garlic, cardamom, allspice, and coriander. Bring to a boil, then reduce to a simmer and cook until the rabbit is cooked through, about 35 minutes (you're looking for an internal temperature of 165°F, similar to chicken). Remove the rabbit and allow it to cool, reserving the stock. Shred the rabbit meat, and discard the bones.

To make the spice mix, combine the cinnamon, allspice, and black pepper in a large bowl. Toss the rabbit meat in the spice mix.

To make the soup, set a large soup pot over medium-low heat. Add the olive oil, onion, and garlic and cook until soft and translucent, 5 to 7 minutes. Add the frozen spinach and kale.

Strain the stock that the rabbit cooked in and add the clear liquid to the pot. Bring to a boil, then reduce the heat and simmer for at least 30 minutes. Season with salt to taste.

Blend slightly with an immersion blender to achieve a smoother texture.

Make the brown butter just before serving. Place the butter, garlic, and coriander in a pot over medium heat. Watch the butter carefully and smell for a nutty aroma. When the milk solids have colored, and the butter is brown, immediately transfer to a bowl to stop the cooking.

To serve, heat a medium pan over medium-high heat and add a splash of olive oil. Add the shredded rabbit to the pan, along with a pinch of salt. Crisp up the rabbit. Place some Egyptian rice in a bowl and then cover with soup. Top with the crispy rabbit and drizzle on the spiced brown butter.

SEARED FALAFEL BURGERS

SERVES 10
PREP TIME: 45 MINUTES
COOK TIME: 30 MINUTES

The best part of the falafel experience is biting into the crispy golden exterior to reveal a bright-green center. That's right, green. A true Egyptian falafel is always green because it is made of fava beans, as opposed to the standard chickpea that most other cultures use. You'll always see an Egyptian break a falafel in half to reveal the color, as if they were the falafel police monitoring authenticity. I make a shortcut version using frozen edamame and peas to save time and give the best color, with no loss of flavor or texture. Then I sear them to make the most crunchy surface and pair them with buttery brioche burger buns. It's the best falafel you'll ever have, or your money back! Just kidding— please don't return this book.

◆

FALAFELS
3 cups frozen shelled edamame
1 cup frozen peas
2 Tbsp all-purpose flour
2 cups parsley, loosely packed
2 cups cilantro, loosely packed
1 cup dill, loosely packed
½ cup mint, loosely packed
½ white onion, minced
2 cloves garlic, minced
1 Tbsp ground cumin
1 Tbsp ground coriander
1 Tbsp caraway seeds
½ tsp chili flakes
1 tsp baking powder
1 tsp salt

TAHINI MAYO
⅓ cup Garlic Mayo, page 209
⅓ cup tahini

For the falafels, preheat the oven to 425°F. Set a large pot of salted boiling water over high heat, and prepare an ice bath. Blanch the edamame and peas in the boiling water for 2 to 3 minutes, then immediately transfer to the ice bath. Drain and dry.

Transfer the edamame and peas to the bowl of a food processor and add the flour, parsley, cilantro, dill, mint, onion, garlic, cumin, coriander, caraway seeds, chili flakes, baking powder, and salt. Pulse until smooth. The falafels should be the consistency of wet sand and keep their shape when you form some into a ball in your hand.

Divide the falafel mix into 10 burgers, then form into patties. Bake in the preheated oven for 16 to 18 minutes or until the tops are golden brown and the burgers are keeping their shape—don't worry about flipping them. This step can be done ahead of time.

To make the tahini mayo, combine the garlic mayo and tahini in a bowl. If the mixture is really thick, add a little cold water to loosen it.

To serve, heat the canola oil in a large pan over high heat. Fry the burgers for 1 to 2 minutes, until the surface is crispy, then flip and fry for another minute. Transfer to a plate and sprinkle with salt to taste.

Toast the brioche buns, making sure not to burn them, then spread mayo on each side of the bun. Layer with a falafel burger, lettuce, tomatoes, turnips, and hot sauce to taste.

TO SERVE

3 Tbsp canola oil

10 brioche buns

1 head romaine lettuce, shredded

4 Roma tomatoes, sliced

2 cups pickled turnips (see note)

Hot sauce, for seasoning

NOTE: Look for bright pink pickled turnips in the international aisle in your local grocery store. Luckily, items like this one are becoming more readily available without having to make a separate trip to any specialty stores.

LEEK KHISK WITH CRISPED KALE AND ONIONS

SERVES 4–6
PREP TIME: 15 MINUTES
COOK TIME: 40 MINUTES

I came across my Teta Aida's khisk soup recipe in a family scrapbook and was surprised that just a handful of ingredients made up such a nuanced flavor profile. This is what my teta was all about, though–making deliciously traditional dishes that were inherently comforting in their simplicity. For this recipe, she bound chicken stock with a mixture of flour and yogurt then finished it with onions and fresh lemon juice. Mine follows the same principle while using half the amount of flour so it's not too thick, and it gets some depth and texture from the leeks and kale. Top it with quick-cooked onions and a sprinkle of smoked paprika for a soup that's pleasantly tangy and rich.

◆

2 large leeks

2 Tbsp butter

2 cloves garlic, minced

4 cups Egyptian Chicken Stock, page 226

1 cup yogurt

½ cup all-purpose flour

1 tsp salt

2 tsp lemon juice

GARNISH

½ bunch kale

4 Tbsp olive oil, divided

Salt

1 white onion, diced

Smoked paprika

1 lemon

Preheat the oven to 350°F and line a baking sheet with parchment paper. Cut the leeks in half lengthwise and wash well under cold water, being careful to rinse out any dirt that may be lodged between the different layers. Slice the leeks thinly, discarding the roots.

In a large pot, heat the butter over medium-low heat. Sweat the leeks and garlic in the butter for 8 to 9 minutes to soften, then add the stock. Bring to a boil, then reduce and simmer for 30 minutes.

To make the garnish, rip the kale into pieces and coat evenly in 2 tablespoons of the olive oil. Place on the baking sheet and bake for 15 to 17 minutes, until crispy. Season with salt to taste.

Heat the rest of the olive oil in a skillet over medium-high heat. Add the diced onions and cook for 3 minutes, until brown.

After the soup has simmered for 30 minutes, mix the yogurt and flour well in a bowl. Add the mixture to the soup and bring back to a boil, whisking well. Reduce the heat to a simmer and cook for another 5 minutes. Season with salt and freshly squeezed lemon juice. The soup can be served as is or pureed. Transfer everything to a blender or use an immersion blender to smooth it out. It doesn't have to be perfectly smooth, but this step is according to your personal preference.

Pour the soup into bowls and garnish with some crispy kale and cooked onions. Sprinkle on some smoked paprika, and add another dash of lemon juice to finish.

FRIED SHRIMP SANDWICHES

SERVES 4
PREP TIME: 20 MINUTES
COOK TIME: 5 MINUTES

Pitas stuffed with fried shrimp are found all over Egypt, from coastal locations like Alexandria and the Suez Canal all the way to fishmongers in Cairo. My recipe has some Canadian influence with the Old Bay finish and the maritime-favored top-cut bun. Nordic shrimp are readily found frozen and already cooked, so it's just a matter of a quick fry, making this dish perfect for summertime entertaining.

◆

12 oz precooked cold-water Nordic shrimp

1 cup cornstarch

1 tsp paprika

1 tsp ground cumin

1 tsp onion powder

¼ tsp chili powder

Vegetable oil, for frying

Large pinch salt

1 cup Garlic Mayo, page 209

2 Tbsp lemon juice

½ head iceberg lettuce, finely sliced

4 top-cut buns (see note)

½ cup Tahini Sauce, page 210

1 tsp Old Bay seasoning

¼ cup finely chopped parsley

2 lemons, cut into wedges

Dash of hot sauce (optional)

Thaw the shrimp overnight in the fridge, or in a bowl of cold water for 10 to 15 minutes. Once thawed, pat the shrimp dry. In a separate bowl, mix together the cornstarch, paprika, cumin, onion powder, and chili powder. Add the shrimp and toss in the dry mix.

In a large pot bring 1½ inches of vegetable oil to 350°F and line a baking sheet with paper towel.

Place some of the shrimp in a spider or small strainer to dust off the excess cornstarch mixture. Transfer the shrimp to the hot oil and fry for 1 minute, flipping them so they brown on all sides. Work in batches so you don't lower the temperature of the oil too much. The shrimp are already cooked, so this step is about quickly getting a golden-brown exterior. Transfer the shrimp to the lined baking sheet and season immediately with a sprinkle of salt. Repeat with the remaining shrimp.

Combine the garlic mayo and lemon juice in a mixing bowl. Add the chopped lettuce and season with a pinch of salt. Toss to combine.

Open each bun and place some of the dressed lettuce in the bottom. Top with some of the fried shrimp, then garnish with a drizzle of tahini sauce, a sprinkling of Old Bay seasoning, some fresh chopped parsley, a squeeze of fresh lemon juice, and a dash of hot sauce.

◆

NOTE: You can substitute whole wheat pitas or Egyptian Whole Wheat Baladi Bread (page 224) for a more traditional sandwich if you like.

YOGURT-BRAISED SHORTRIB SHAWARMA

SERVES 6

PREP TIME: 20 MINUTES, PLUS
4–8 HOURS FOR MARINATING

COOK TIME: 3 HOURS
20 MINUTES

1 cup kefir or plain yogurt

½ cup + 3 Tbsp olive oil, divided

1 tsp hot sauce

1 tsp ground cumin

1 tsp ground coriander

1 tsp allspice

1 Tbsp smoked paprika

1 tsp onion powder

1 tsp garlic powder

1 tsp cinnamon

1 tsp black pepper

4 lb beef short ribs, bone in

Salt, for seasoning

2 quarts beef stock

2 white onions

1 tsp sumac

¼ cup finely chopped parsley

1 head iceberg lettuce

3 Roma tomatoes

1½ cups pickled turnips

1 cup sliced dill pickles

1 cup Lebanese Toum, page 213

1 cup Tahini Sauce, page 210

6 large pitas, or 18 mini pitas

Hot sauce, for seasoning

Replicating an amazing shawarma at home can be tough, especially if you don't have a giant spit and a 100-pound stack of meat, but this recipe can help! You can use chicken thighs, beef, or lamb here. This is a great meal or appetizer for a cocktail party, if served on mini pitas.

◆

Whisk together the kefir, ½ cup of the olive oil, the hot sauce, cumin, coriander, allspice, smoked paprika, onion powder, garlic powder, cinnamon, and black pepper in a large nonreactive bowl. Place the short ribs in the marinade and refrigerate for at least 4 hours, or preferably overnight.

Remove the short ribs and wipe off the excess marinade, reserving the marinade. Season the meat generously with salt on all sides.

Preheat the oven to 350°F and set a Dutch oven over medium-high heat. Heat the remaining 3 tablespoons of olive oil and sear the short ribs on all sides. Work in batches if necessary to avoid overcrowding. Remove the beef after searing and deglaze the pot with the stock. Add the short ribs back to the pot, and add about 1 cup of the marinade. Cover the pot with a tight-fitting lid and set in the oven. Braise for 3 hours or until the short ribs are fall-apart tender.

While the meat cooks, prep your veggies. Finely slice the onions and toss with the sumac and parsley. Allowing them to sit together will mellow the sharpness from the onion a bit. Finely slice your lettuce, tomatoes, pickled turnips, and dill pickles and prepare the toum and tahini sauces.

Once the beef has braised, remove the short ribs and pull the meat off the bones. Strain the braising liquid (the kefir will have separated somewhat, which is totally normal).

Line a baking sheet with aluminum foil and place the shredded meat on top. Add 1 cup of the braising liquid, and broil on high for 2 minutes, watching carefully. You want to deeply brown and caramelize the beef to mimic the direct heat from a shawarma spit, but you don't want to burn it.

Line each pita with a dollop of toum, then fill with lettuce, tomatoes, onions, turnips, and pickles. Top with some of the beef, then drizzle with tahini sauce and hot sauce to taste.

MOM'S RED LENTIL SOUP

SERVES 6
PREP TIME: 15 MINUTES
COOK TIME: 1 HOUR

This soup checks a lot of boxes—it's comforting, healthy, and hearty enough to be a meal. It's also easy to make: it uses a few simple ingredients that you probably have kicking around your kitchen at all times. Make a batch on a cold weekend night and save the rest for later in the week. Like many soups, it tends to get even better after a day or two.

◆

1 onion, minced

2 cloves garlic, minced

2 stalks celery, diced

2 Tbsp olive oil

1 tsp ground cumin

½ tsp cinnamon

3 roma tomatoes, chopped

1 cup red lentils

6 cups beef or vegetable stock

½ tsp salt

GARNISH

⅓ cup whipping cream

⅓ cup olive oil

1 lemon, zested

Pale celery leaves from the inner bunch

In a large pot over medium-low heat, sweat the onion, garlic, and celery in the olive oil for 5 minutes. Add the cumin and cinnamon and toast for an additional minute. Add the tomatoes, lentils, stock, and salt. Bring to a boil then reduce to a simmer and cook for 45 minutes, or until all of the veggies and lentils are soft.

Transfer to a blender or use an immersion blender to process to your desired texture.

Divide the soup into 6 bowls and garnish each bowl with a drizzle of cream, a drizzle of olive oil, a little lemon zest, and a few bright-green celery leaves.

◆

NOTE: Always save those pale-green leaves on the inside of your celery stalks. They have a bright, fresh flavor and are a beautiful garnish on a soup or salad. Avoid the dark-green leaves as they can be somewhat bitter.

MANAKEESH WITH LAMB AND YOGURT

SERVES 6–8
PREP TIME: 1 HOUR, PLUS
2 HOURS 30 MINUTES FOR RISING
COOK TIME: 10 MINUTES

Almost every culture has some form of flatbread, and Middle Eastern cuisine is no different. Really, this dish could have been called several different names. Basically, it's a simple pizza dough topped with a za'atar spread, seasoned lamb and some fixings. No cheese here, but if you added some to enter officially into pizza land, I think that would be pretty fun too.

◆

FLATBREAD

2 tsp active dry yeast
8 cups "00" or all-purpose flour
3 tsp salt
1 Tbsp sugar
1 Tbsp olive oil

ZA'ATAR SPREAD

¼ cup fresh thyme
¼ cup sesame seeds
2 Tbsp dried mint
1½ Tbsp sumac
1½ Tbsp aniseed
2 tsp dried orange (optional)
1 tsp chili flakes
1½ tsp salt
1¼ cups olive oil

LAMB

1 lb ground lamb
1 tsp salt
1 tsp cinnamon

TOPPING

2 red onions, finely sliced
1½ cups plain yogurt
1 bunch mint leaves

To make the flatbread, place 1 cup of warm water in a bowl, then sprinkle on the yeast to bloom. Wait 10 minutes, until the yeast has foamed.

Place the flour, salt, sugar, and olive oil in the bowl of a stand mixer. Then add the yeast and water. Add 1 cup + 2 tablespoons of water to the bowl. Using the dough hook attachment, knead on medium speed until the mixture forms a smooth ball, about 10 minutes.

Place the dough in a lightly oiled bowl and cover loosely with a tea towel. Allow to rise for 1½ hours or until doubled in size.

Return the dough to your work surface. Divide evenly into 4 pieces, then form into balls by pinching the four corners together and rounding off. Transfer the balls to a baking sheet and proof at room temperature, loosely covered, for another hour (or overnight in the fridge for a more complex flavor). The balls can be used after the proofing or individually wrapped and frozen.

Preheat the oven to 450°F.

To make the za'atar spread, combine the thyme, sesame seeds, dried mint, sumac, aniseed, dried orange, chili flakes, salt, and olive oil. For the lamb, mix the lamb meat with salt and cinnamon in a separate bowl.

Roll out each dough ball into a rough oval shape about ¼-inch thick. Spread some of the za'atar mixture on each piece of dough. For the topping, add dollops of the lamb, and slices of onion. Bake for 10 minutes on an unlined baking sheet, until the dough is golden and the lamb meat has cooked. Remove and allow to cool for 1 to 2 minutes. Top with dollops of yogurt and mint leaves.

BEEF HAWAWSHI SANDWICHES

SERVES 4–6
PREP TIME: 15 MINUTES
COOK TIME: 15 MINUTES

This Cairo street food staple is simple and versatile—a must-have for your sandwich repertoire. Baking the beef mixture and sandwich together marries the flavors and allows the rendered fat to crisp up the pita. If you don't want to bake your own Egyptian Whole Wheat Baladi Bread (page 224), or can't find the true Egyptian pita (check your local Middle Eastern grocer and ask for baladi bread), just substitute whole wheat pitas instead.

◆

½ green pepper

½ white onion

2 cloves garlic

½ bunch parsley

¼ bunch cilantro

¼ bunch mint leaves

1 lb ground beef

1 Tbsp smoked paprika

1 tsp ground coriander

1 tsp salt

½ tsp cinnamon

¼ cup Harissa, page 211

3 loaves Egyptian Whole Wheat Baladi Bread, page 224

1 cup Tahini Sauce, page 210

Hot sauce, for seasoning

Preheat the oven to 425°F and line a baking sheet with parchment paper.

Finely dice the green pepper, onion, garlic, parsley, cilantro, and mint. Place in a large mixing bowl along with the beef, paprika, coriander, salt, cinnamon, and harissa. Mix well.

Cut the baladi bread in quarters, then fill with the meat mixture. Place on the baking sheet and cook for 15 minutes, until the meat is cooked through and the bread is crispy. Serve with a side of tahini and a dash of hot sauce.

CHICKPEA AND TOMATO HALABISSA SOUP

SERVES 4–6

PREP TIME: 10 MINUTES, PLUS OVERNIGHT FOR SOAKING

COOK TIME: 2 HOURS 40 MINUTES

1 cup dried chickpeas, soaked overnight

3 Tbsp olive oil

1 white onion, finely diced

3 cloves garlic, finely minced

2 pints grape tomatoes

1 tsp ground cumin

1 tsp ground aniseed

¼ tsp allspice

¼ tsp black pepper

½ tsp salt

⅓ cup tomato paste

4 cups Egyptian Chicken Stock, page 226

1 lemon

I sometimes struggle to find vegetarian entrées that are satiating, but this soup fits the bill. It's packed with protein, nutrients, and flavor—the ideal meatless meal on a cold day. And as I say with most soups, enjoy some the next day for lunch when it's even tastier!

◆

Soak the chickpeas overnight in the fridge in a large bowl, covered by at least a few inches of cold water. The longer you soak the chickpeas, the easier they will be to cook the next day, so try to soak them for 8 to 12 hours.

Strain the chickpeas and place them in a large pot. Cover them again with cold water and a pinch of salt. Bring to a boil, then reduce to a simmer and cook for 45 to 60 minutes. Be sure to skim the skins that rise to the top during cooking. When the chickpeas are cooked, you'll be able to smash one easily between your fingertips. Strain the chickpeas and set aside.

In a large pot or Dutch oven, heat the olive oil over medium-low heat. Add the onions and garlic, and cook for 4 to 5 minutes, until softened but not too colored. Add the grape tomatoes and increase the heat to medium-high. Cook for 2 to 3 minutes to blister the tomatoes so they start to release their juices. Add the cumin, anise, black pepper, and salt, and cook for another 1 to 2 minutes. Add the tomato paste and cook for 1 minute, before adding the stock. Bring the soup to a boil, then reduce the heat to low and simmer for 1½ hours, until the soup has reduced and deepened in color and the edges of the pot are golden brown. To serve, ladle the soup into bowls and finish with a squeeze of bright lemon juice and an extra drizzle of olive oil.

ALEXANDRIA-STYLE CALF LIVER ON TOAST

SERVES 4

PREP TIME: 30 MINUTES, PLUS 4 HOURS FOR SOAKING

COOK TIME: 15 MINUTES

Though my dad is from Cairo, he has nostalgic memories of Egypt's favorite coastal city, Alexandria. He would spend summers there in the 50s and 60s when it was a world-class Mediterranean destination. My theory is that this soft spot for Alex has led to his bizarre relationship with liver, which happens to be a key ingredient in one of the city's standard street sandwiches. You see, anytime he's in a restaurant or pub with liver on the menu he orders it, then immediately says: "You know, I don't even like liver." If you don't like liver, use steak, and top it with this amazing green pepper relish.

◆

1 lb calf liver

2 cups milk

3 cloves garlic, smashed

2 bay leaves

Salt and pepper, for seasoning

1 cup all-purpose flour

3 Tbsp olive oil

3 Tbsp butter, divided

2 pints cherry tomatoes

8 slices country bread

2 limes, cut in wedges

GREEN PEPPER RELISH

3 Tbsp olive oil

1 green pepper, finely chopped

1 green chili, finely chopped

1 red chili, finely chopped

½ onion, minced

1 clove garlic, minced

½ tsp salt

1 Tbsp sugar

1 lime, juiced

Soak the liver in the milk with the garlic and bay leaves for at least 4 hours. This will mellow out the flavor of the liver.

To make the green pepper relish, heat the olive oil in a large pan set over medium-high heat. Add the green pepper, red and green chilies, onion, and garlic, and cook for 2 to 3 minutes. Add the salt and sugar, and cook for an additional minute. Finish with lime juice to keep the flavors bright. This is a quick cook, as we want the relish to still have some bite to it. Transfer to a bowl.

Pat the liver dry, then season with salt and pepper. Place the flour in a shallow dish, and dredge the liver in the flour, shaking off excess.

In a large pan over medium-high heat, heat the olive oil until it ripples, just before smoking. Cook the liver for 2 minutes on the first side, then 1 minute on the flip side. Liver should be cooked to medium, as over-cooking turns it grainy and gray.

Remove the liver from the pan, then take the pan off the heat to cool slightly, draining off any excess oil. Reduce the heat to medium, then return the pan to the heat and add 2 tablespoons of butter and the tomatoes. Cook for 3 minutes, so the tomatoes soften and release their juices. Season with salt to taste. In a separate pan, toast the bread with the remaining tablespoon of butter. To serve, top the bread with tomatoes, then slice the liver and place over the tomatoes. Finish with a spoonful of the green pepper relish and fresh lime on the side.

BEEF SAMBOUSEK

SERVES 8–10

PREP TIME: 1 HOUR, PLUS
1 HOUR 30 MINUTES FOR RISING

COOK TIME: 40 MINUTES

These little meat pies mean a lot to my mom, as my teta would always make her a big batch every time she was studying for one of her pharmacy exams. I like to make them in a small snack size, and I always make a big batch and freeze a few for later. Feel free to mix up the meat (the beef here is traditional, but you can get creative with any ground meat that you choose) and master this dough for your go-to bun recipe.

◆

DOUGH

1⅓ cups + 1 Tbsp milk

1¼ tsp active dry yeast

¼ cup sugar, divided

3¼ cups all-purpose flour

1½ tsp salt

⅓ cup cold butter, cubed

MEAT FILLING

1 onion, minced

2 cloves garlic, minced

2 Tbsp olive oil

1 lb ground beef

1 Tbsp tomato paste

1 tsp salt

1 tsp ground coriander

½ tsp cinnamon

¼ tsp chili powder

¼ cup pine nuts, finely chopped

½ cup finely chopped parsley

1 egg

Tahini Sauce, page 210, for serving

Hot sauce, for serving

Begin by making the dough. Warm the milk to 110°F by gently heating it in a small pot on your stovetop. If you don't have a thermometer, check the temperature with your finger: the milk should feel warm to activate the yeast but not so hot that it's uncomfortable to hold your finger in it for more than a few seconds. Take the milk off the heat. Sprinkle the yeast and half of the sugar into the warm milk and stir gently. Allow to sit for about 10 minutes, or until the yeast begins to foam at the surface of the milk.

Mix the flour, salt, and remaining sugar together in the bowl of a stand mixer. Then, using the dough hook attachment, add the milk mixture and mix on medium speed for 4 to 5 minutes. Add the cubed butter, a few pieces at a time. Mix for another 10 to 15 minutes until the dough forms a ball that separates cleanly from the sides of the mixing bowl. Have patience with this process. At the beginning the dough will look too wet, but if you spend the time to develop the gluten and strengthen the dough, it will eventually form a perfect ball.

Place the dough in a lightly oiled bowl and cover loosely with a tea towel. Allow to rise at room temperature for 1½ hours, or in the fridge overnight, until it has roughly doubled in size.

To make the meat filling, place a large pan over medium-low heat. Sweat the onion and garlic in the olive oil for 3 to 5 minutes, until softened but not too colored. Add the beef, tomato paste, salt, coriander, cinnamon, and chili powder and cook on medium-high heat for 7 to 8 minutes or until the beef is cooked through, stirring regularly. Add the pine nuts and parsley last to preserve their color and slight crunch. Stir, then remove from the heat and allow to cool completely.

continued on p. 96

Divide the dough into small evenly sized pieces (depending on how big you would like your meat pies to be). I find that this recipe makes about 22 to 24 mini meat pies. Dust your work surface with some additional flour to prevent sticking, then roll out each small piece of dough into a circle.

Preheat the oven to 375°F and line two baking sheets with parchment paper. Place a small mound of the meat mixture in the middle of each rolled-out piece of dough, then brush some water on the top edge to help the edges seal. Fold the bottom edge up and gently press down to prevent air pockets as you seal the dough and crimp the edges with a fork.

Place the meat pies on the baking sheets. Add a splash of water to the egg and whisk it in a small bowl. Use a pastry brush to paint each meat pie with a bit of egg wash for color. Bake the meat pies for 25 to 27 minutes, until they're golden brown. Serve with tahini and hot sauce on the side.

◆

NOTE: Making the dough, preparing the meat filling, and baking the pies is a bit of work, so it's nice to know that you can freeze an inventory of these delicious snacks for when you need them. Freeze them in a single layer on a baking sheet, and cover tightly with plastic to prevent freezer burn. Once completely frozen, you can store them on top of each other in a resealable container, then reheat them in a hot oven when ready to serve.

SPICY TURKEY FETEER

SERVES 6–8

PREP TIME: 30 MINUTES, PLUS
RESTING TIME FOR THE DOUGH

COOK TIME: 40 MINUTES

This feteer (a layered dough that can be filled with savory or sweet ingredients) is about to take over pizza night at my house. Unlike trying to create great pizza, which is hard with a home oven, you'll find that these feteers easily become crispy and delectable, the ideal vehicles for a variety of meat or veggie fillings. I opted for ground turkey for a bit of a leaner version and embraced the seasonings of a traditional sausage to keep the flavors bold.

◆

1 batch Feteer Dough, page 222, divided into 4 balls

SPICY TURKEY FILLING

1¼ cups + 1 Tbsp olive oil, divided

1 white onion, diced

4 cloves garlic, finely minced

1½ lb ground turkey

1½ Tbsp ground fennel

1½ Tbsp smoked paprika

3 tsp chili flakes

1½ tsp salt

⅓ cup tomato paste

1½ cups chicken stock

3 Tbsp cold butter, cubed

TO ASSEMBLE

¼ cup butter

3 tsp olive oil

Make your feteer dough and allow to rest. This can be done the day before, as the dough is much easier to work with after it rests in the fridge overnight.

Make the turkey filling by heating 3 tablespoons of the olive oil in a large frying pan over medium-low heat. Add the onion and garlic, stirring regularly for 5 to 6 minutes. Then add the turkey and increase the heat to medium-high. Cook for another minute, stirring so that all of the ground meat can break up and begin to cook. Add the fennel, smoked paprika, chili flakes, and salt and cook for another 1 to 2 minutes, still stirring regularly. Add the tomato paste and cook for an additional minute, followed by the stock. Bring to a boil and then reduce to a simmer and cook for 5 to 6 minutes. Break up all of the meat and allow the liquid to cook away. Finish by turning off the heat and swirling in the cold butter.

Transfer the meat mixture to a food processor and blitz a few times. You're not trying to make a meat puree; you're just making the consistency of the whole mixture easier to spread on the feteer dough. Transfer the mixture to a bowl, and whisk in the remaining olive oil.

To assemble, flatten out a ball of the feteer dough by gently pressing it against your work surface, as if you're carefully flattening out a ball of pizza dough. With your fingers, coax the dough from the edges to become thinner and thinner. You should be left with a wide, thin circular piece of dough.

continued on p. 98

Remix the turkey and oil mixture if need be, then spread a quarter of the mixture in the center of the dough with a spatula. Fold one side into the middle of the dough, then repeat in a circular motion until all of the sides have reached the center. The dough will form a wheel shape, enclosing the meat filling.

Preheat the oven to 375°F and line a baking sheet with parchment paper. In a cast-iron skillet, heat 1 tablespoon of the butter with 1 teaspoon of the olive oil over medium heat. Add the feteer, folded side up and cook for 3 minutes, until the bottom is nicely browned. Flip and cook for another minute or so, then transfer to the baking sheet. Repeat with the remaining feteers, adding more butter and oil as needed. Transfer the sheet pan of feteers to the oven and bake for 25 minutes. Remove, cut into quarters, and enjoy!

◆

NOTE: If you don't have a cast-iron skillet, you can cook the feteers at a higher temperature (425°F) for the same 25 minutes, also with delicious results.

FIVE-HOUR "SHORTCUT" BASTURMA

SERVES 4
PREP TIME: 5 MINUTES
COOK TIME: 5 HOURS

I know what you're thinking: "Five hours is a shortcut?" Fair point, but consider this: a traditional basturma (which is essentially a Middle Eastern pastrami) is cured for up to two weeks! By finding premade corned beef, you save yourself the time and trouble of curing the meat, and you're still able to apply your own spice blend for the authentic basturma flavor. Considering how long it takes, feel free to store the beef in your fridge, then just slice and reheat it with some water in a pan whenever you crave a mouthwatering hot sandwich.

◆

2 lb corned beef
1 Tbsp ground fenugreek
1 Tbsp smoked paprika
½ Tbsp black pepper
½ Tbsp ground coriander
¾ tsp ground cumin
¼ tsp chili flakes
3 cloves garlic, minced
8 slices rye bread
½ cup yellow mustard

Preheat the oven to 235°F. Rinse the corned beef very well under cold water to remove any leftover curing spices and dry completely with paper towel.

In a bowl, mix the fenugreek, smoked paprika, black pepper, coriander, cumin, chili flakes, and garlic, then rub the spice mixture all over the meat, massaging on all sides.

Wrap the beef tightly in foil, then wrap again in another layer of foil to create a tight package. Place on a baking sheet, then transfer to the oven for 5 hours.

Remove the beef from the oven. You can slice the beef and enjoy right away, or let it cool and keep it in your fridge for up to 4 days.

To reheat, slice the beef into ½-inch-thick pieces and heat them in a pan with some water until the water evaporates and the beef is warm. Serve between slices of rye bread, slathered with tangy mustard.

SALADS
AND SIDES

HEIRLOOM TOMATO FATTOUSH SALAD

SERVES 4
PREP TIME: 25 MINUTES

The perfect fattoush has the right balance of parsley, tomatoes, radishes, greens, and of course, crispy pita. I've doubled down on the parsley here by saucing the bottom of the plate with a vibrant parsley sauce that's easy and versatile. Also, if you can't find watermelon or breakfast radishes, don't worry—normal radishes will look and taste great. And lastly, the sumac pita chips in the recipe are dangerously addictive. Make some extra just for snacking.

◆

PARSLEY SAUCE

2 cups parsley, loosely packed (about 1 bunch)

1 cup buttermilk

½ tsp salt

SUMAC PITA CHIPS

2 pitas

1 Tbsp olive oil

1 tsp sumac

½ tsp salt

SALAD

1 pint heirloom baby tomatoes

½ red onion

3 baby cucumbers

2 watermelon radishes

2 breakfast radishes

2 heads romaine

½ cup Basic Lemon Vinaigrette, page 209

Salt and pepper, for seasoning

To make the parsley sauce, place the parsley, buttermilk, and salt in a blender. Blend until incorporated and bright green. This is best made the day of serving to preserve its amazing color.

To make the pita chips, preheat the oven to 400°F and line a baking sheet with parchment paper. Cut the pitas into 1-inch squares, then coat with olive oil, sumac, and salt. Roast for 10 to 12 minutes, until golden brown and crunchy. You've been warned though, so maybe double down on this recipe and have some ready for snacking.

To assemble the salad, halve the tomatoes to reveal their beautiful color. Finely slice the onion, cucumbers, and radishes. A mandoline is a great tool for this task, but watch your fingers! Otherwise a sharp knife does the job. Finely slice the romaine. Place everything in a bowl. Pour the lemon vinaigrette around the bowl until the ingredients are just coated. A perfectly dressed salad isn't soggy! Season to taste with salt and pepper. Place dollops of the parsley sauce on each plate, then place a serving of salad overtop. Top with the pita chips and enjoy.

SUMMER GREEN BEAN FASOLIA

SERVES 6
PREP TIME: 15 MINUTES
COOK TIME: 45 MINUTES

Traditional fasolia is an Egyptian side dish made of green beans braised in tomato and spices, and it's a dish that I remember well from my childhood. My only complaint was that despite the vibrant nature of each ingredient, everything inevitably ended up quite *brown*. I wanted to make a version that kept these inherently summery ingredients bright green and red—respecting the memory of the dish, but reimagining the look and texture. My mom always topped her version with slivered almonds, so as a nod to her, I toasted some and crushed them on top for a nostalgic garnish.

◆

3 red onions, roughly cut

4 cloves garlic, minced

2 Tbsp olive oil

1½ tsp Ras el Hanout, page 215

¼ cup tomato paste

3 beefsteak tomatoes, grated

1½ cups beef stock

3 Tbsp cold butter

1 cup almonds

¾ lb green beans, trimmed

1½ Tbsp olive oil

¼ tsp salt

In a saucepan over medium-low heat, soften the onion and garlic in the olive oil for 3 to 4 minutes, stirring regularly. Add the ras el hanout and toast lightly for an additional minute. Add the tomato paste and cook for another 1 to 2 minutes. Add the grated tomatoes and beef stock and bring to a boil. Lower the heat and simmer for 20 minutes. When the sauce has reduced by two-thirds, swirl in the cold butter. Keep warm.

Preheat the oven to 375°F. Place the almonds on a baking sheet and toast for 7 to 8 minutes in the oven, until lightly golden and aromatic. Allow to cool and then coarsely chop and set aside.

Increase the oven temperature to 425°F. Toss the green beans with the olive oil and salt. Place them in a single layer on an unlined baking sheet and roast for 14 to 16 minutes. The green beans should get some color and have a slight al dente bite still.

Serve by placing the tomato sauce on the bottom of your platter. Top with the roasted green beans, then sprinkle on the toasted almonds.

SPICED RICE AND YELLOW ZUCCHINI MAHSHI

SERVES 4–6

PREP TIME: 20 MINUTES,
PLUS TIME FOR COOLING

COOK TIME: 1 HOUR

The term *mahshi* can be used to described any vegetable, such as zucchinis, tomatoes, or bell peppers, stuffed with rice and/or meat. I always enjoyed the zucchini version, filled with well-seasoned rice and cooked in bright tomato sauce. In this recipe, I cook the rice separately so that I can control the cooking time of the zucchinis a bit better, leaving the vegetable with just enough bite.

◆

SPICED RICE

1 cup basmati rice

3 Tbsp olive oil

1 white onion, minced

4 cloves garlic, minced

1 tsp oregano

1 tsp sumac

1 tsp allspice

1 tsp cinnamon

1 tsp turmeric

1 tsp paprika

1 tsp salt

½ tsp chili powder

⅓ cup tomato paste

2 cups vegetable stock

1 Tbsp butter

¼ bunch dill, finely chopped

¼ bunch parsley, finely chopped

STUFFED ZUCCHINIS

4 yellow zucchinis

1½ cups passata

½ cup vegetable stock

4 roma tomatoes, chopped

2 Tbsp olive oil

Pinch salt

To make the spiced rice, first wash all of the starch off the rice. Place the rice in a strainer and run under cold water, then transfer to a bowl of cold water. Allow the rice to sit for a few minutes before repeating the process again. Repeat 3 to 4 times until the water is clear and no longer foggy from the starch—this will take about 20 to 25 minutes in total. Drain the rinsed rice.

In a pot, heat the olive oil over medium-low heat, then add the onion and garlic. Sweat for 3 to 4 minutes, stirring regularly. Next, add the oregano, sumac, allspice, cinnamon, turmeric, paprika, salt, and chili powder and cook for another minute to bring out the aromas. Add the tomato paste and cook for an additional minute. Add the rinsed rice, stock, and butter, then bring to a boil over medium-high heat. Reduce to a low simmer, then cover and cook for 17 to 20 minutes until the liquid is absorbed. Take the pot off the heat and let the rice sit for 5 minutes, before opening the lid and fluffing with a fork. Fold in the fresh dill and parsley, then allow to cool before stuffing the zucchinis.

To make the stuffed zucchinis, preheat the oven to 425°F. Halve the zucchinis lengthwise and carefully hollow out the flesh with a spoon (you can save this part for a soup or stock). Spoon the rice into the hollowed-out zucchinis. Fill a roasting pan with the passata, vegetable stock, and the tomatoes. Place the stuffed zucchinis overtop and drizzle on the olive oil along with a pinch of salt. Roast for 35 minutes. Remove and serve with some of the tomato sauce from the bottom and spoon on any rogue rice that may have fallen out!

THREE PEPPER BALADI SALAD

SERVES 4

PREP TIME: 25 MINUTES

A baladi, or simple country salad, is a basic staple in Egyptian cuisine. When making a composed salad like this, always consider the role that each ingredient plays. The radicchio's bitterness offsets the sweetness of the peppers, the sunflower seeds add some crunch, and the quinoa makes this a satisfying side or even a light lunch.

◆

1 red pepper, finely diced

1 yellow pepper, finely diced

1 orange pepper, finely diced

2 mini cucumbers or ½ English cucumber

¼ head radicchio, finely sliced

1 shallot, diced

1 cup cooked quinoa, cooled

½ cup Basic Lemon Vinaigrette, page 209

¾ tsp salt

1 Tbsp finely chopped parsley

1 Tbsp finely chopped cilantro

½ cup feta, crumbled

2 Tbsp sunflower seeds

In a large mixing bowl, combine all of the peppers, the cucumbers, radicchio, shallot, and quinoa. Drizzle the dressing around the outer edge of the bowl and season with salt. Lightly toss all of the ingredients in the dressing right before serving. Place the salad on a serving platter and garnish with the parsley, cilantro, crumbled feta cheese, and the sunflower seeds.

FIRE-ROASTED SWEET POTATOES WITH ALEPPO PEPPER AND HONEY BUTTER

SERVES 4–6
PREP TIME: 5 MINUTES
COOK TIME: 1 HOUR 20 MINUTES

I once watched a chef bury sweet potatoes in hot coals until they were blackened on the outside and exceptionally soft on the inside. The orange flesh of the potato was a bright pop of contrast with the black exterior, and it was smoky and delicious. I told my mom about it, and she remembered street vendors in Egypt who would serve the same thing—slow-roasted sweet potatoes that she gobbled up during her student days. Here I've baked the potatoes to cook them through and then finished them on an open flame to achieve the same look and smoky taste.

◆

4 sweet potatoes
¼ cup butter, softened
1½ tsp wildflower honey
Salt, for seasoning
1 tsp Aleppo pepper
¼ bunch chives, finely sliced

Preheat the oven to 400°F and line a baking sheet with parchment paper. Scrub and dry the potatoes, then poke holes all over each one. Wrap each potato in aluminum foil and place them on the baking sheet. Bake from 60 to 75 minutes, depending on the size, until they're very soft and tender. If a sharp knife goes in easily, they're done.

While the potatoes cook, mix the butter and honey together.

When the potatoes are done, remove and discard the foil, then place each potato over an open flame on your cooktop or barbecue. Cook for 2 to 3 minutes, turning occasionally, so that the entire exterior is blackened while the interior absorbs the smoky flavor. Transfer the potatoes to a serving dish, cut each one in half lengthwise, and score the surface. Spread the honey butter overtop and season liberally with salt, Aleppo pepper, and chives. Remember not to eat the blackened outside!

◆

NOTE: You can bake the potatoes and char them on the grill just before serving, if you'd like to make them ahead.

MO'AMAR RICE WITH MUSHROOMS AND TRUFFLES

SERVES 6–8
PREP TIME: 35 MINUTES
COOK TIME: 25 MINUTES

1 cup Calrose rice

1½ cups milk

1 cup Egyptian Chicken Stock, page 226

½ cup whipping cream

¾ tsp salt

2 Tbsp olive oil

1 Tbsp butter

4 oz cremini mushrooms, sliced

4 oz shiitake mushrooms, sliced

25–30 g fresh truffles, shaved (see note)

This Egyptian rice dish is like combining a baked pilaf with a creamy risotto, all in one foolproof pot. As long as you make sure to rinse the short-grain Calrose rice well, you'll end up with a decadent and addictive result. You can add your favorite spices to this dish, but I decided to keep mine basic, leaving a blank canvas for the stock, mushrooms, and the fancy truffles to complement the rich rice.

◆

The first key step is to wash all of the starch off the rice. Place the rice in a strainer and run under cold water, then transfer to a bowl of cold water. Allow the rice to sit for a few minutes before repeating the process again. Repeat 3 to 4 times until the water is clear and no longer foggy from the starch—this will take about 20 to 25 minutes in total. Washing off all of this starch is an important step for the final texture of the rice.

Preheat the oven to 375°F. Place a Dutch oven over medium-high heat, then add the rinsed rice, milk, stock, cream, and salt. Bring to a boil then transfer to the oven. Bake, uncovered, for 18 to 20 minutes, until the top begins to brown and the rice is cooked.

While the rice is in the oven, sauté the mushrooms. In a large skillet over high heat, heat the olive oil and butter. Add the sliced cremini and shiitake mushrooms along with a pinch of salt, and leave undisturbed in a single layer. Allow the mushrooms to get some nice caramelization, then stir and continue to cook out their water content, 5 to 6 minutes.

Remove the rice from the oven, then spoon on the mushrooms. Lastly, shave the fresh truffles overtop and serve to your lucky guests.

◆

NOTE: You only need 3 to 5 grams of truffle per person, but it's not unheard of to pay upward of $5 per gram, so try to befriend a local restaurant truffle supplier who is willing to make a house call. If you can't find truffles, finish this version of mo'amar with a drizzle of quality truffle oil on top right before serving.

ROASTED EGYPTIAN POTATOES WITH ONIONS AND PEPPERS

SERVES 6
PREP TIME: 15 MINUTES
COOK TIME: 35 MINUTES

My mom's potatoes were classic—peeled and roasted in a casserole with onions, peppers, and tomato sauce. My version has the same DNA, but a sear and roast at an extremely high temperature gives that deep browning that I love so much. Who knows, maybe my mom will start to make her potatoes using my recipe? Well I doubt that, but nothing is stopping you!

◆

½ cup tomato paste

½ cup + 2 Tbsp olive oil, divided

2 tsp ground cumin

1 tsp chili flakes

1 tsp salt

2 lb yellow potatoes, about 2 inches in diameter, or fingerling potatoes

2 white onions, cut into 1-inch chunks

2 red peppers, cut into 1-inch strips

Preheat the oven to 450°F. Mix the tomato paste, ½ cup of the olive oil, cumin, chili flakes, and salt together in a large mixing bowl.

Peel the potatoes and add them to the bowl, followed by the white onions and peppers. Toss in the seasoned tomato paste mixture.

Heat the remaining olive oil in a large heavy-bottomed or cast-iron skillet over medium-high heat. Pick the potatoes out of the mixing bowl and sear them for 2 to 3 minutes to brown, making sure to rotate them to get color on all sides. Add the rest of the onions, peppers, and tomato paste mixture to the skillet and transfer to the oven. Roast for 30 minutes to cook through and get a deeper coloration. Remove from the oven and enjoy!

SEARED HALLOUMI AND ORANGE-GLAZED BEET SALAD

SERVES 4

PREP TIME: 15 MINUTES

COOK TIME: 2 HOURS
15 MINUTES

Halloumi is a versatile semi-hard white cheese that has been prominent in Middle Eastern and Greek cooking for generations and with good reason—it can be seared, grilled, or even broiled. It gives a dish that salty punch that is sometimes needed to elevate the other players in a salad. As for the beets, always roast them (never boil!) and glaze them in a little bit of reduced orange juice for flavor and shine together with a little residual red juice to drizzle on the plate for a beautiful finish.

◆

½ lb red beets

½ lb yellow beets

½ cup orange juice

1 cup baby arugula

¼ cup Basic Lemon Vinaigrette, page 209

Salt and pepper, for seasoning

4 slices country bread

2 Tbsp olive oil, divided

2 Tbsp pistachios, finely chopped

4 oz halloumi, sliced

Preheat the oven to 400°F and line a baking sheet with aluminum foil. Wrap the red beets together tightly in aluminum foil and then do the same with the yellow beets in a separate foil wrapping. Roast in the oven for 1½ to 2 hours until tender. Peel the beets while still warm, then chop them into 1½-inch pieces. Leave the oven on.

Place the red beets in a large pot over medium-high heat along with the orange juice, and reduce for 2 to 3 minutes until the consistency is syrupy. Note that we're only reducing the red beets in the orange juice here—adding the yellow beets will sacrifice their contrasting color.

Toss the yellow beets and arugula in the vinaigrette until evenly coated and season with salt and pepper to taste (use sparingly, the halloumi is quite salty).

Drizzle the bread with 1 tablespoon of the olive oil and toast in the hot oven for 5 to 8 minutes until golden and crispy.

Heat the remaining tablespoon of olive oil in a nonstick skillet on medium heat. Place the slices of halloumi in the hot pan and sear for 1 to 2 minutes per side, until golden brown. Place slices of halloumi on each plate and surround with the beets and arugula. Top with chopped pistachios and crispy bread, and drizzle the remaining orange juice reduction around each plate.

TOMATO-GLAZED EGGPLANT WITH BROILED CREAM

SERVES 3–4
PREP TIME: 20 MINUTES
COOK TIME: 1 HOUR

I have an extremely serious confession to make. This is a safe place, right? OK, here it goes—I have never *loved* eggplant. Growing up, my mom would do what most Egyptian mothers do with eggplant and prepare it like a Greek moussaka. Her baked version, covered in tomato and béchamel, had such a monotonous texture that it reminded me more of baby food than anything else. But this dish is a staple in Egyptian cuisine so I was determined to give it another shot. Here, I glaze my eggplants and roast them at a pretty high temperature, yielding sweet and crispy skin while achieving a creamy interior. I also like to cook the sauce separately and then broil the whole dish with this simple white sauce on top for some extra richness.

◆

½ cup tomato paste

¼ cup brown sugar

1 chili, minced

1 clove garlic, minced

1 tsp ground cumin

1 tsp ground coriander

1 eggplant

2 Tbsp olive oil

Large pinch salt

Chunky Egyptian Tomato Sauce, page 223

Chives, minced, for garnish

WHITE SAUCE

½ cup sour cream

¼ cup whipping cream

¼ cup grated pecorino Romano

Preheat the oven to 435°F and place a wire rack on a baking sheet that's been lined with aluminum foil.

In a saucepan, combine the tomato paste, brown sugar, ½ cup water, chili, garlic, cumin, and coriander. Bring to a boil, then reduce the heat and simmer for 5 to 8 minutes to thicken slightly.

Cut the eggplant into ½-inch rounds. Using a pastry brush, paint the glaze all over each piece of eggplant. Place the coated eggplant on the wire rack, drizzle on some olive oil, and season with salt. Roast for 45 to 50 minutes, or until the edges have crisped and the eggplant flesh is cooked and creamy.

To make the white sauce, whisk together the sour cream, cream, and pecorino. Season with a pinch of salt.

Place the tomato sauce on the bottom of a large ovenproof skillet or roasting pan. When the eggplant has cooked, remove from the oven and place on top of the tomato sauce. Dollop some white sauce on each piece of eggplant, then broil for 1 minute to get some color. Top with minced chives. Enjoy!

FINGERLING POTATO SALAD WITH BELUGA LENTILS AND LABNEH

SERVES 6
PREP TIME: 20 MINUTES
COOK TIME: 55 MINUTES

Basic potato salads were a fixture at all my family functions, especially in the summer. Depending on the mom in charge, there may or may not have been green lentils in the mix, but the crowd seemed to be indifferent to their addition or omission. The right choice of lentil, however, can make or break a potato salad! I like the sturdier black variety of lentil, for better flavor and texture. A little touch of spice, along with bright lemon, parsley, and tang from the labneh will make this a hit at your next barbecue.

◆

1½ lb fingerling potatoes
¼ cup beluga lentils
3 Tbsp olive oil
1 Tbsp lemon juice
½ tsp ground cumin
¼ tsp chili powder
1 clove garlic, finely minced
½ white onion, finely diced
1 tsp salt
¼ bunch parsley, finely chopped
½ cup Labneh with Garlic Confit, page 217

Place the potatoes in a large pot and cover with cold water by 2 inches. Bring to a boil, then reduce to a simmer. Cook until the potatoes are fork-tender, about 30 minutes, then strain.

Allow to cool slightly, but peel away the skins of the potatoes with your hands while they're still warm (it's much easier with a little bit of heat remaining).

In a small pot, cover the lentils with ¾ cup water and a pinch of salt. Bring to a boil, then reduce to a simmer. Cook for about 25 minutes, or until the lentils are tender, but with an al dente bite. Strain any remaining liquid and allow to cool.

Slice the cooked, peeled, and cooled potatoes into coins or lengthwise, depending on your preferred presentation. Then, place the potatoes in a large mixing bowl and add the oil, lemon juice, cumin, chili powder, garlic, onion, and salt. Fold gently so as to not crush the potatoes, then fold in the cooked cooled lentils as well. Lastly, fold in the fresh parsley and top with dollops of the garlic labneh.

GRILLED BABY ARTICHOKES WITH TOMATO BÉCHAMEL AND GARLIC CRISPS

SERVES 3–4

PREP TIME: 20 MINUTES

COOK TIME: 25 MINUTES

12 baby artichokes

1 lemon

2 Tbsp olive oil

Salt and pepper, for seasoning

TOMATO BÉCHAMEL

2 Tbsp butter

2 Tbsp flour

1 cup milk

1 cup passata

Pinch salt

GARLIC CRISPS

4 cloves garlic, thinly sliced

⅓ cup olive oil

GARNISH

1 lemon, zested and squeezed

2 Tbsp grated pecorino Romano

One of my mom's holiday specials was a hollowed-out artichoke heart, filled with meat and served with tomatoes and thick béchamel. I wanted my version to serve as a light vegetarian side dish that was easier to prepare while still reflecting the flavor that I grew up with. If you can't find baby artichokes, a high-quality canned variety will work. Just make sure to wash them off and dry them well.

◆

Fill a bowl with cold water and cut the lemon into wedges. Squeeze some of the lemon juice into the water to prevent the artichokes from browning.

Prepare the baby artichokes by cutting off the tip of the top, trimming the stems, and peeling away the tough, dark-green outside layers. Immediately place each artichoke in the lemon water before moving on to the next.

Transfer the artichokes along with the lemon water to a large pot. Bring to a boil, then reduce the heat and simmer for about 10 minutes or until tender.

To make the tomato béchamel, melt the butter in a pot, then add the flour. Stir the butter and the flour with a wooden spoon to keep lumps from forming in the corners of the pot. Cook for 1 to 2 minutes, then add the milk and passata. Bring to a boil, whisking constantly, and cook for 2 to 3 minutes, until the sauce is slightly thickened. Season with a pinch of salt and keep warm.

To make the garlic crisps, place the sliced garlic and olive oil in a small pan and cook over medium heat for 3 to 4 minutes, until the garlic becomes golden brown. Keep a close eye on this so the garlic doesn't burn. Remove the garlic with a slotted spoon and place on a plate lined with paper towel.

Remove the artichokes from the pot and place in bowl of ice water to stop the cooking. Once cooled, remove each baby artichoke and cut it in half to expose its layered interior. Drizzle with olive oil and season with a pinch of salt and pepper.

Grill the artichoke halves on medium-high heat for 1 to 2 minutes. You can do this either on a barbecue, in a grill pan, or even by sautéing them in a skillet.

To serve, put some of the tomato béchamel on the bottom of your platter and top it with the grilled artichokes. Add some of the garlic crisps, then finish with lemon zest and juice, and some grated pecorino to finish.

BRAISED RAINBOW CHARD WITH TARO CHIPS

SERVES 4–6
PREP TIME: 20 MINUTES
COOK TIME: 45 MINUTES

Traditionally in Egyptian cuisine, taro is stewed with Swiss chard to make a soup. But to me, taro is best when it's crisped up in a hot oven, yielding a crispy golden chip that serves as the perfect complement to the soft braised chard. While this recipe might be a far cry from the authentic version, I think the flavors honor its history. Complete it with some pickled chard stems for acidity, and it all adds up to a killer side dish.

◆

1 medium-sized taro root

6 Tbsp olive oil, divided

½ tsp salt

1 bunch rainbow chard, sliced, stems reserved

3 cloves garlic, minced

½ red onion, minced

1 Tbsp ground coriander

¼ tsp chili powder

3 cups chicken stock

1 Tbsp butter

¼ bunch cilantro, chopped

2 Tbsp + 1 tsp lemon juice

½ tsp sugar

Preheat the oven to 400°F and line a baking sheet with parchment paper.

Peel the taro root, then thinly slice it using a mandoline or a very sharp knife—try to keep the slices even. Place the slices on the baking sheet. Drizzle 3 tablespoons of the olive oil and sprinkle a pinch of salt overtop, and mix with your fingers to coat the taro pieces. Roast for about 20 minutes, until golden brown. These taro chips can be made ahead and stored in an airtight container for up to 3 days.

Cut the chard leaves away from the stems, reserving the stems for pickling. Thinly slice the leaves.

In a large frying pan set over medium-low heat, heat the remaining 3 tablespoons of olive oil and add the garlic, onion, and a pinch of salt. Sweat, stirring regularly, for 3 to 4 minutes. Add the coriander and chili powder to toast for an additional minute. Add the sliced rainbow chard and increase the heat to medium-high. Cook, stirring consistently, for 1 to 2 minutes. Add the chicken stock, bring to a boil, then reduce to a low simmer. Cook for 18 to 20 minutes, until the stock has reduced to approximately ¾ cup and the chard has softened nicely. Finish with the butter, cilantro, and a squeeze of lemon juice, about 1 teaspoon. Taste and add another pinch of salt if necessary.

While the chard leaves cook, pickle the stems. Slice the chard stems into evenly sized pieces, then place them in a large skillet with ½ cup water, the sugar, and the remaining 2 tablespoons of lemon juice. Bring to a boil, then reduce to a simmer. Cook for about 5 minutes, until all of the liquid has cooked off and the stems are softened and cooked through.

To plate, place the braised chard on a large dish, topped with the pickled stems. Add the taro chips right before serving to keep them crispy.

VINEGAR-GLAZED TURNIPS WITH DUKKAH

SERVES 6
PREP TIME: 20 MINUTES
COOK TIME: 40 MINUTES

I wanted to make pickled turnips a star side dish as opposed to the ubiquitous little bowl that's often forgotten at the edge of the table. This recipe cooks the turnips with beets to give them that spike of pink, and the vinegar glaze provides the tang without taking upward of a week as traditional pickling does. The final touch of the onion, dukkah, and dill take this dish to the next level.

◆

6 medium-sized turnips
4 medium-sized red beets
4 cloves garlic
2 bay leaves
⅔ cups red wine vinegar
⅓ cup white vinegar
2 Tbsp sugar
1 white onion, thinly sliced
2 Tbsp olive oil
Pinch salt
⅔ cup Dukkah, page 218
¼ bunch dill, chopped

Peel the turnips and cut them into 1-inch pieces. Peel the beets next and cut them into similar-sized pieces.

Place the turnips and beets in a pot and cover with cold salted water. Add the garlic and bay leaves, and bring to a boil. Reduce the heat to a simmer and cook for 30 to 35 minutes, until the turnips and beets are tender. Strain the vegetables and discard the garlic and bay leaves.

Add the beets and turnips back to the pot and cover with the red wine vinegar, white vinegar, and sugar. Cook for an additional 5 to 6 minutes until the vinegar and sugar have reduced almost completely and have glazed the turnips and beets. Remove the turnips and beets from the pot and allow to cool completely.

When ready to serve, place the thinly sliced white onion on a plate. Top with the turnips and beets, then drizzle on the olive oil along with a generous pinch of salt to taste. Top with the dukkah and dill.

DEHYDRATED TOMATO AND PARSLEY TABBOULEH SALAD

SERVES 4–6
PREP TIME: 25 MINUTES
COOK TIME: 2 HOURS

Letting tomatoes hang out in a low-temperature oven is a tremendous way to amplify their natural sweetness. I use this technique not just for salads like this one, but also when I want to use the tomatoes for pasta or on grilled bread. Aside from that, this tabbouleh couldn't be simpler and makes for a refreshing side dish or light summer entrée.

◆

2 pints cherry tomatoes

4 cloves garlic, minced

1 bunch parsley

2 Tbsp olive oil

⅓ cup fine bulgur

1 batch Basic Lemon Vinaigrette, page 209

½ English cucumber, diced

½ bunch mint, picked

½ bunch scallions, finely sliced

Salt, for seasoning

Preheat the oven to 250°F and line 2 baking sheets with parchment paper. Slice the cherry tomatoes in half and place them on one baking sheet, along with the garlic. On the second baking sheet, place one-quarter of the parsley to be dehydrated as well. Drizzle the tomatoes and garlic with some olive oil, then place both baking sheets in the oven. Take out the parsley after 1 hour, then remove the tomatoes after dehydrating for an additional hour (2 hours in total).

Place the bulgur in a bowl and cover with ⅔ cup warm water. Cover tightly with plastic wrap and let sit for 30 minutes. Remove the plastic wrap and fluff the bulgur with a fork. Allow to cool completely before assembling the salad.

In a medium bowl, blend approximately one-third of the tomatoes with the lemon vinaigrette.

Finely chop the remaining fresh parsley and place in a large mixing bowl. Add the rest of the dehydrated tomatoes, the cooled bulgur, and the cucumber, mint, and scallions. Season with salt to taste, then drizzle some of the dressing around the outer rim of the bowl. Gently fold all of the ingredients together and dress just to coat.

To serve, add a little extra tomato dressing on the bottom of the plate. Place the dressed salad on top. Scatter some dehydrated parsley leaves throughout, and crush some between your fingers to season parts of the salad with parsley powder.

BLISTERED OKRA WITH GREEN SAUCE AND BAKED CHEESE

SERVES 6
PREP TIME: 15 MINUTES
COOK TIME: 25 MINUTES

Almost every vegetable in Egyptian cooking is cooked in some form of tomato sauce, and that goes for okra too. I wanted to explore something different when it came to this polarizing vegetable, and luckily my mom told me about this coriander and chard sauce that they sometimes serve with it. So for this recipe I use my go-to trick to avoid "slimy" okra (high heat!), pair it with this vibrant sauce, then finish the dish with some spice from the chili and umami crunch from the baked cheese crisps.

◆

GREEN SAUCE

¼ cup + 2 Tbsp olive oil, divided

1 white onion, diced

4 cloves garlic, minced

1 bunch green Swiss chard trimmed and roughly chopped

¼ tsp + pinch salt

1 bunch cilantro

1 Tbsp lemon juice

GARNISH

½ cup grated pecorino Romano

1 chili, finely sliced

OKRA

3 Tbsp olive oil

1 lb okra

Pinch salt

½ cup beef stock

1 Tbsp lemon juice

Begin by making the green sauce. Place a large skillet over medium heat. Add 2 tablespoons of the olive oil, then the onion and garlic. Cook for 3 to 4 minutes, stirring regularly. Add the chard to the skillet, along with a pinch of salt, and increase the heat to high. Cook for another 1 to 2 minutes, allowing the chard to wilt.

Bring a separate pot of salted water to a boil, and have a bowl of ice water waiting. Remove a few cilantro stems from the bunch and set aside for garnish. Drop the remaining cilantro bunch into the boiling water and blanch for approximately 30 seconds. When the water returns to a boil after the cilantro is dropped in, it's a good sign that the cilantro has cooked long enough. Remove immediately and shock in the ice water to cool and preserve the bright-green color.

In a blender, combine the blanched cilantro with the cooked Swiss chard mixture. Add the remaining ¼ cup olive oil, lemon juice, ½ cup water to loosen, and the ¼ tsp salt. Blend until well incorporated and set aside.

For the garnish, preheat the oven to 375°F and line a baking sheet with a nonstick silicone baking mat or parchment paper. Place the grated cheese on the prepared baking sheet in an even layer. Bake for 4 to 5 minutes until the cheese melts and becomes golden. Remove and allow it to cool completely so that it crisps up.

To make the okra, heat the olive oil on high in a cast-iron skillet. Once the oil is very hot (almost smoking), add the okra and allow to blister and char. Turn the okra when needed, and season with a pinch of salt. Cook on high heat for 5 to 6 minutes. Add the stock and allow to cook further and reduce for another 2 to 3 minutes. Turn off the heat and drizzle with the fresh lemon juice.

To serve, place some of the green sauce on the bottom of the plate, then arrange the okra on top. Scatter some of the chili slices and reserved cilantro leaves on top, and break up pieces of the crispy cheese.

◆

NOTE: You can use a regular skillet to cook the okra, but cast iron is the best for retaining heat to get that great sear. It's definitely worth the investment and the extra steps needed for care, and these skillets will last a lifetime if properly looked after.

TRIPLE-SESAME CARROTS WITH GOAT CHEESE

SERVES 6
PREP TIME: 10 MINUTES
COOK TIME: 45 MINUTES

Roasted carrots get enhanced with three different sesame applications—sesame seeds, black tahini, and a unique savory halva. The slight bitterness of the black tahini serves as the counterbalance to the sweetness of the carrots, but feel free to substitute plain tahini if you can't find black tahini. I like to use smaller, heirloom-sized carrots for this recipe—but you can use larger ones if you like. Just be sure to roast them a bit longer until they are cooked through and fork-tender.

◆

2 lb carrots

2 Tbsp olive oil

2 Tbsp butter

2 tsp salt

¼ cup sesame seeds

BLACK TAHINI SAUCE

⅓ cup black tahini (see note on page 43)

1 Tbsp lemon juice

¼ tsp salt

GARNISH

½ cup crumbled goat cheese

½ cup Not Too Sweet, Not Too Spicy Halva, crumbled, page 229

½ bunch parsley, finely chopped

Preheat the oven to 425°F. Peel and wash the carrots, making sure to dry them well, which will allow a nice sear.

Heat the oil and butter in a large skillet over medium-high heat, then add the carrots and sprinkle on the salt. Sear for 3 to 4 minutes, turning periodically to get deep coloration all around the carrots. Add the sesame seeds, and stir to coat evenly.

Transfer to the oven and roast for 40 to 45 minutes, until the carrots are fork-tender.

To make the black tahini sauce, mix the black tahini and lemon juice, then loosen with a small amount of water if needed. Finish with the salt.

To garnish, plate the carrots with some of the black tahini sauce, then top with a sprinkle of the goat cheese and halva. Finish with fresh parsley and enjoy.

MAIN PLATES

TETA AIDA'S KOFTA

SERVES 4

PREP TIME: 15 MINUTES

COOK TIME: 10 MINUTES

My Teta Aida was the classic grandma who would cook from the heart. Her kofta, like most of her cooking, was simple but always well seasoned. With spices like cinnamon and allspice, you want to include just enough so that you know they're there, but not so much that you're overwhelmed by them. Here, I've swapped out beef for bison for an interesting and lean flavor profile, but feel free to swap it back. Or get creative with any other ground meat. If you use this ratio of spices, you'll be hard-pressed to mess it up.

◆

½ lb ground bison

½ lb ground lamb

½ white onion, grated

2 cloves garlic, minced

½ bunch parsley, finely chopped

1 tsp salt

1 tsp cinnamon

½ tsp allspice

¼ cup breadcrumbs

2 pitas, quartered

1½ cups Cucumber and Garlic
   Yogurt, page 210

2 cups Egyptian Rice, page 212

Preheat the oven to 400°F and line a baking sheet with parchment paper.

Combine the bison, lamb, onion, garlic, parsley, salt, cinnamon, allspice, and breadcrumbs in a large bowl, being careful not to overmix. Form into small ovals and bake for 10 minutes in the preheated oven.

Remove the kofta from the oven and serve with pita bread, cucumber and garlic yogurt, and Egyptian rice.

◆

NOTE: You can also skewer the kofta and grill them for 3 to 4 minutes per side if you don't want to bake them.

MULBERRY-GLAZED DUCK WITH GINGER AND CHERRY FREEKEH

SERVES 6
PREP TIME: 20 MINUTES
COOK TIME: 2 HOURS
40 MINUTES

While freekeh can be a bit tough to find (I buy mine at a local health food store), it's worth the search. Freekeh is produced by an ancient method of roasting and rubbing green durum wheat, and is usually used as a stuffing for chicken or squab in Egyptian cuisine. For this recipe, I like to cook the freekeh separately with aromatic ingredients while slow-roasting the duck before glazing it with mulberry molasses—another distinctly Middle Eastern item to look out for.

◆

Preheat the oven to 350°F.

DUCK AND GLAZE

6 duck legs

Pinch salt

⅔ cup mulberry molasses (see note)

¼ cup white wine vinegar

1½ tsp cinnamon

½ tsp chili flakes

FREEKEH

2 Tbsp olive oil

½ white onion, minced

2 cloves garlic, minced

1 celery stalk, diced

1 Tbsp grated fresh ginger

½ tsp cinnamon

½ tsp ground cumin

½ tsp ground coriander

1 cup cracked freekeh (see note)

½ cup dried cherries

1½ cups chicken stock

1 orange, zested and juiced (about 1 cup)

½ tsp salt

½ cup parsley, finely chopped

To make the duck, place the duck legs in a shallow baking dish with a pinch of salt, and cover well with foil. Roast for 2 hours.

Combine the mulberry molasses, vinegar, cinnamon, and chili flakes in a small pot and bring to a boil, stirring occasionally. Remove from the heat.

To make the freekeh, in a large pot set over medium-low heat, heat the olive oil, then sweat the onion, garlic, celery, and ginger for 4 to 5 minutes. Add the cinnamon, cumin, and coriander and increase the heat to medium, cooking for another minute or so. Add the freekeh, dried cherries, stock, orange juice, and salt. Bring to a boil, then reduce to a simmer and cook, covered, for 22 to 24 minutes until the liquid has been absorbed and the freekeh is tender. Remove from the heat and let sit for 5 minutes. Stir in the orange zest and parsley to finish.

Remove the duck from the oven. Increase the oven temperature to 425°F and place a wire rack on a baking sheet. Place the duck legs on the rack and season with a pinch of salt. Roast for 10 minutes, then remove from the oven. Using a pastry brush, paint the glaze on each of the legs. Return to the oven for an additional 10 minutes.

Reheat the freekeh if necessary. Spread on a platter, or on individual plates, then top with the glazed duck.

NOTE: You can buy whole or cracked freekeh, but I prefer the latter because of the texture and shorter cook time. Even though this recipe has a specific cook time, refer to the cooking instructions on whatever package of freekeh you do find, as timing can vary. If you can't find freekeh, you can substitute bulgur, quinoa, or rice, but adjust your cooking time accordingly.

Look for mulberry molasses in a Middle Eastern grocery store. If you can't find any, try pomegranate molasses, which is more readily available, instead. Also look for dried mulberries in your bulk food store, as they make a fun garnish and a great snack as well.

GRILLED WHOLE FISH WITH YELLOW PEPPER VINAIGRETTE AND CHARRED SCALLIONS

SERVES 2

PREP TIME: 30 MINUTES

COOK TIME: 10 MINUTES

2 sea bream or sea bass fish, about 1 lb each, cleaned

¼ bunch cilantro

1 lemon, sliced

¼ cup olive oil

Salt and pepper

YELLOW PEPPER VINAIGRETTE

1 yellow pepper, finely diced

3 cloves garlic, finely minced

1½ tsp ground cumin

1½ tsp smoked paprika

¼ tsp salt

1 lemon, juiced

½ cup + 2 Tbsp olive oil

½ bunch cilantro, finely chopped

GARNISH

1 bunch scallions

2 Tbsp olive oil

Salt and pepper

2 lemons

Simply grilled whole fish is ubiquitous in Egyptian coastal cities. Grilling a fish whole offers several key benefits: bone-in cooking always offers the most flavor, stuffing the cavity with aromatics infuses the fish with lemon and herbs, the skin crisps and crackles delightfully against the soft flesh, and, lastly, it looks really cool. When buying whole fish, talk to your fishmonger to make sure it's fresh. Ask them to clean and gut the fish for you too, saving you the trouble at home.

◆

Remove the fish from the fridge and dry each side very well with paper towel. You want the skin to crisp on the grill and not steam and stick. Stuff the cavity of each fish with a few sprigs of cilantro and a few slices of lemon and allow the fish to come to room temperature on a baking sheet, about 30 minutes.

To make the vinaigrette, in a bowl, combine the pepper, garlic, cumin, smoked paprika, and salt. Add the lemon juice and olive oil and whisk well to emulsify. Mix in the cilantro.

Once the fish is at room temperature, heat a grill or grill pan to high heat. Drizzle about 1 tablespoon of olive oil on each side of the fish and season with salt and pepper to taste. Wipe the grill down with some oil as well to keep the skin from sticking. Grill the fish on the first side for about 3 minutes. Flip carefully (use tongs and try to grip from the head—this will hopefully avoid tearing the crisped skin) and cook for another 2 to 3 minutes. Remove and allow to rest for 1 to 2 minutes.

For the garnish, toss whole scallions in some olive oil and season with salt and pepper. Char on high heat for 2 to 3 minutes, turning occasionally. At the same time, you can halve and char the lemons for 2 to 3 minutes. Place the scallions on the bottom of your serving platter. Top with the grilled fish, then spoon on the vinaigrette. Serve with the charred lemons for squeezing.

ARABIC COFFEE AND CORIANDER BEEF RIBS WITH POMEGRANATE BARBECUE SAUCE

SERVES 3–4

PREP TIME: 15 MINUTES

COOK TIME: 3 HOURS 30 MINUTES

My friend Shai introduced me to this incredible idea: rubbing beef with equal parts coffee and coriander, with a pinch of sugar. I've been using this rub for years, but the tweak of using Arabic coffee brings in a subtle hint of cardamom as well. Look for ground Arabic coffee in a specialty Middle Eastern grocery store, or substitute by adding a pinch of cardamom to your favorite coffee. This recipe features a rib cooking technique that you can use for beef, pork, and even lamb ribs. Plus, the pomegranate barbecue sauce is another go-to that you can rely on all grilling season.

◆

1 Tbsp coriander seeds, toasted and ground

1 Tbsp ground Arabic coffee

½ tsp sugar

½ tsp chili flakes

2 lb beef back ribs

POMEGRANATE BARBECUE SAUCE

2 Tbsp olive oil

3 cloves garlic, minced

½ white onion, minced

1 Tbsp minced fresh ginger

1 tsp paprika

1 tsp cinnamon

½ tsp chili flakes

1 cup ketchup

½ cup balsamic vinegar

¼ cup pomegranate molasses

⅓ cup brown sugar

½ tsp salt

3 Tbsp olive oil, for grilling

Preheat the oven to 300°F. Mix the coriander, coffee, sugar, and chili flakes in a small bowl. Rub the seasoning all over the ribs and massage into the meat. Wrap the beef ribs tightly in foil, then wrap again in another piece of foil. This tight wrapping helps to trap the heat and steam, allowing the ribs to cook slowly and become fall-apart tender. Place on a baking sheet in the oven and cook for 3 hours.

To make the barbecue sauce, heat the olive oil in a pot over medium-low heat. Sweat the garlic, onion, and ginger in the oil for 8 to 10 minutes, until soft and translucent. Add the paprika, cinnamon, and chili flakes and cook for an additional minute, then add the ketchup, vinegar, pomegranate molasses, brown sugar, salt, and 1 cup water. Bring the sauce to a boil, then simmer over very low heat for 25 to 30 minutes, until darkened and thickened. This sauce can be made several days in advance.

Remove the ribs from the oven and unwrap. They should be fork-tender and almost falling off the bone. Coat the ribs in the sauce.

Heat some olive oil in a grill pan over medium-high heat. Season the ribs with a generous pinch of salt and place on the grill pan. Grill for 1 to 2 minutes per side to caramelize the sauce, but be mindful not to burn the sugars. Remove, carve individual ribs for serving, and enjoy!

GRILLED CORNISH HEN WITH LEMON AND BLACK CUMIN

SERVES 2–4

PREP TIME: 20 MINUTES, PLUS 4 HOURS FOR MARINATING

COOK TIME: 25 MINUTES

2 Cornish hens

2 lemons, juiced

½ cup olive oil

1 Tbsp honey

1 Tbsp Dijon mustard

½ tsp ground cumin

½ tsp ground coriander

½ tsp cinnamon

¼ tsp chili flakes

3 cloves garlic, minced

¼ bunch parsley, finely chopped

SPICE MIX

1½ tsp black peppercorns

1 tsp cumin seeds

1 tsp coriander seeds

1 tsp black cumin seeds (or kalonji/nigella)

3 Tbsp olive oil, for grilling

2 lemons, for squeezing

Small birds like Cornish hens and squabs are typically stuffed in Egyptian cuisine, but I far prefer breaking them down into two halves and grilling them. This gives me the chance to marinate them and char the outside. If you can't find Cornish hens, substitute half chickens. It's worth the effort to find black cumin seeds for this dish, as finishing the hens with an additional sprinkling provides a distinctly herbaceous flavor and striking aesthetic.

◆

Place each Cornish hen breast side up on a cutting board. Using a small paring knife, score the hen in the neck area to expose and remove the little wishbone. Next, flip the hen so that the breast side is down and the backbone is facing you. Using kitchen shears, cut along each side of the backbone and remove it. You can now flatten the hen (it's basically spatchcocked at this point). Flip it over and score the breast plate to remove it easily before cutting the hen in half. You can leave each half bone in at this point, or work your knife along the remaining bones to separate the breast meat while leaving the bones in the leg and thigh.

In a large mixing bowl, whisk together the lemon juice, olive oil, honey, mustard, cumin, coriander, cinnamon, chili flakes, garlic, and parsley. Add the hens to the marinade, and cover tightly with plastic wrap. Transfer to the fridge and marinate for at least 4 hours and up to overnight.

To make your spice mix, toast the peppercorns, cumin seeds, coriander seeds, and black cumin seeds in a dry pan over medium heat. The aromas will start to wake up and the seeds will begin to crackle slightly.

Place the spices in your spice grinder and pulse a few times (or crush on a cutting board with the back of a skillet). Don't turn the spices into a fine powder—the mix should keep some texture. Transfer the spice mix to a bowl.

Preheat the oven to 400°F and line a baking sheet with parchment paper. Place the Cornish hens on the baking sheet. Season each side with a generous sprinkling of the spice mix and a pinch of salt.

Heat the olive oil on medium-high in a grill pan and place the hens in the pan, skin side down. Cook undisturbed for 1 to 2 minutes, until the hens release easily from the pan and the skin is crispy and brown. Flip and spoon on some of the marinade, cooking for another 30 seconds.

Transfer the hens back to the baking sheet and place in the oven. Roast for 18 to 20 minutes, until the hens are cooked through (the internal temperature should reach 165°F) but still juicy and tender.

Place the cooked hens on a platter and sprinkle on another generous pinch of the spice mix. Serve with lemon wedges, as a fresh hit of lemon juice at the very end of the cooking process really makes these spices sing!

VEAL CHOP BOFTEK WITH KOHLRABI AND POMEGRANATE SALAD

SERVES 2
PREP TIME: 15 MINUTES
COOK TIME: 10 MINUTES

I'll never forget being served a crispy and delicious schnitzel at a family party in my childhood. I asked the host, my mom's friend Mervat, what it was. "Brain," she said. Ha! I laughed aloud and asked again. She looked at me seriously and confirmed "brain." Well, this recipe isn't brain, because the Egyptian people bread and shallow-fry cutlets of all sorts, including veal. I made this version with a pounded-out, bone-in veal chop for a dramatic presentation. Feel free to use the same recipe with a boneless cutlet of veal, chicken, turkey . . . or some brain if you're brave enough. For the record, I never ate at Mervat's house again.

◆

1½ cups all-purpose flour

2 eggs

1 cup panko breadcrumbs

1 cup fine breadcrumbs

1½ Tbsp za'atar, plus extra for garnish

Two 14 oz bone-in veal chops

¼ cup olive oil

1 Tbsp butter

KOHLRABI AND POMEGRANATE SALAD

2 Tbsp Basic Lemon Vinaigrette, page 209

1 tsp pomegranate molasses

Pinch salt

1 head kohlrabi, julienned

1 cup parsley, loosely picked

½ cup pomegranate seeds

Preheat the oven to 425°F and set up a dredging station. Place the flour in one bowl, the eggs in another, and mix the breadcrumbs and za'atar in a third.

Flatten the veal chop by placing it between two layers of plastic wrap. Pound around the bone and flatten the meat to about ½-inch thickness. Then dredge the veal in the flour, shaking off the excess, followed by the egg, then the breadcrumbs. Repeat with the second veal chop.

Heat the olive oil and butter in a large frying pan over medium-high heat. Place the veal in the pan and cook for 2 to 3 minutes, until it's a deep golden brown. Flip and cook for 1 more minute, then place in the oven for 3 to 4 minutes until cooked to medium. Season with a pinch of salt and then rest for at least 5 minutes.

To make the salad, in a serving bowl, mix the lemon vinaigrette with the pomegranate molasses and salt. Add the kohlrabi, parsley, and pomegranate seeds. Top with the crispy veal and an additional sprinkling of za'atar.

BRAISED BEEF CHEEK BIL BASAL

SERVES 4
PREP TIME: 20 MINUTES
COOK TIME: 3 HOURS
10 MINUTES

2½ lb beef cheeks, cleaned and cut into 3-inch pieces (see note)

2 tsp onion powder

Salt and pepper

3 Tbsp olive oil

6 cloves garlic, minced

16 oz pearl onions, peeled (about 4 cups)

¾ cup dry red wine

⅓ cup tomato paste

3 cups beef stock

½ bunch thyme

½ bunch rosemary

3 bay leaves

3 cups Egyptian Rice, page 212

This Egyptian braise is all about beef, onions, and time. I opted for the criminally underrated beef cheek, which, when braised, is tender and just as flavorful as any other low-and-slow cut. Ask your butcher specifically for the cheeks, and they will automatically know that you know what's up. The second star of this show is the pearl onions, but feel free to substitute a white onion cut into large pieces.

◆

Be sure to ask your butcher to clean the beef cheeks of any sinew. Pat the cheeks dry with paper towel and preheat the oven to 300°F. Season the beef with the onion powder, along with a large pinch of salt and pepper.

Heat the olive oil in a Dutch oven set over medium-high heat. Sear the beef cheeks for 2 to 3 minutes, making sure to brown them on all sides. Transfer the beef cheeks to a plate. Turn the heat to low and wait for 1 to 2 minutes. When the heat has subsided a bit, add the garlic, onions, and a pinch of salt. Cook on low for 1 to 2 minutes, making sure to stir and scoop up some brown bits from the bottom. Add the wine, tomato paste, beef stock, thyme, rosemary, and bay leaves. Increase the heat and bring to a boil, making sure to scrape up any brown bits remaining on the bottom. Add the beef cheeks and cover. Place in the oven and braise for 3 hours.

Remove from the oven and enjoy as a stew, perfect with a side of Egyptian rice. You can reduce some of the braising liquid to make for a thicker sauce as well.

◆

NOTE: You may need to call your butcher a few days in advance so that they can save you those prized beef cheeks, but it's worth the planning. They are not only delicious, but an affordable cut as well. If you're stuck and can't get beef cheeks in time, you can substitute a beef short rib. Also note that the flavor of this dish gets better with time, so feel free to braise the cheeks a day or two in advance and then reheat them.

ROASTED COD SAYADIEH WITH COUSCOUS AND PAN SAUCE

SERVES 4
PREP TIME: 10 MINUTES
COOK TIME: 25 MINUTES

An authentic sayadieh is a fish fillet with rice, usually served with tomato and toasted nuts. I wanted to create a weekday version that could be cooked in about half an hour, with big flavors and bold colors. So, I've swapped the rice for a simple couscous and dusted the cod with seasoned flour before searing it and finishing it in the oven quickly. Topped with a pan sauce, pine nuts, and some ras el hanout, this is an impressive and affordable fish dish that belongs in your weekly rotation.

◆

COUSCOUS
1 cup couscous
1 tsp ground cumin
1 tsp turmeric
1 tsp salt
1 clove garlic, minced
¼ cup + 2 Tbsp olive oil, divided
1½ Tbsp lemon juice
¼ bunch chives, finely sliced

ROASTED COD
1 lb cod loin
¼ cup all-purpose flour
2 tsp Ras el Hanout, page 215
3 Tbsp canola oil
Salt

PAN SAUCE
½ pint grape tomatoes, sliced
¼ cup dry white wine
1 tsp Ras el Hanout, page 215
3 Tbsp cold butter, cubed
1 tsp lemon juice
¼ bunch parsley, finely chopped
Salt

GARNISH
2 Tbsp pine nuts, toasted and finely chopped
1 tsp Ras el Hanout, page 215

Place the couscous, cumin, turmeric, salt, garlic, and 2 tablespoons of the olive oil in a bowl and mix well. Top with 1½ cups boiling water, then cover tightly with plastic wrap to trap the steam. Let the couscous sit for 10 minutes, covered, to absorb the water. Remove the plastic wrap and fluff with a fork. Drizzle in the remaining ¼ cup olive oil, along with the lemon juice and chives.

For the cod, make sure your fish is at room temperature before cooking.

Combine the flour and ras el hanout in a bowl and mix well. Coat each piece of cod in the flour mixture, dusting off any excess.

In a large ovenproof skillet, heat the oil over medium-high heat. When the oil is hot, season the fish with salt then place in the skillet. Cook for 2 to 3 minutes on one side, creating a golden crust. Flip and transfer to the oven for 6 to 8 minutes. Remove from the oven, then take the fish out of the pan and keep warm.

For the pan sauce, pour off any excess oil from the pan. Place over high heat, add the tomatoes, and cook for 1 to 2 minutes. Add the wine and ras el hanout and reduce for 1 minute. After the sauce has reduced by about half, take off the heat and swirl in the butter to emulsify. Finish with the lemon juice, parsley, and salt to taste.

To serve, place the couscous on a platter. Top with the fish, followed by the sauce and some of the pine nuts. Finish with one more sprinkling of ras el hanout and enjoy.

BAKED SUMAC WINGS WITH PARSLEY HOT BUTTER

SERVES 2–3
PREP TIME: 10 MINUTES
COOK TIME: 1 HOUR 5 MINUTES

Tangy sumac is often paired with chicken, especially with the dark and fattier cuts, as the ground sumac berries offer an acidity that counterbalances the richness of the dark meat. Also, this weird technique of slowly rendering the wings and then cranking the temperature—along with adding baking soda (a trick I recently learned on TV!)—gives you a shockingly crispy result. This will become your go-to baking option for making wings at home.

◆

2 Tbsp sumac
1 Tbsp baking powder
1 tsp dried parsley
½ tsp chili flakes
½ tsp garlic powder
½ tsp onion powder
2 lb chicken wings, split
Pinch salt

PARSLEY HOT BUTTER
¼ cup butter, cubed
2 tsp hot sauce
2 tsp dried parsley

GARNISH
2 tsp sumac
1 lemon

Preheat the oven to 250°F. In a large mixing bowl, combine the sumac, baking powder, parsley, chili flakes, garlic powder, and onion powder. Mix well. Add the wings and toss in the dry rub to coat evenly.

Place a wire rack over a baking sheet, then place the wings on top. Bake for 40 minutes. Remove and increase the oven temperature to 450°F. Return the wings to the oven and bake for 25 minutes. Remove the wings again and season with a pinch of salt.

For the parsley hot butter, place the butter, hot sauce, and parsley in a large saucepan over medium-low heat. Swirl constantly to melt the butter, about 1 minute. Once melted, add the wings and increase the heat to medium. Cook for another 30 seconds or so to coat the wings in the butter sauce.

To garnish, transfer to a platter and top with a dusting of sumac and a squeeze of lemon.

KOSHARY WITH RED LENTIL RAGÙ

SERVES 6
PREP TIME: 20 MINUTES
COOK TIME: 2 HOURS
15 MINUTES

Arguably the national dish of Egypt, this is a street-food concoction of pasta, rice, chickpeas, caramelized onions, and lentils, all smothered in a spicy tomato sauce. Years ago, I had this dish in Cairo and went the next two days without having to eat. That said, this version is a bit lighter and channels my Italian restaurant days by saucing the pasta evenly, creating a ragù out of the lentils, and finishing with a good amount of the tangy dakka.

◆

CARAMELIZED ONIONS
1 Tbsp butter
1 Tbsp olive oil
5 onions, sliced
1 tsp salt

CRISPY CHICKPEAS
One 26 oz can chickpeas, rinsed
3 Tbsp olive oil
¼ tsp chili powder
½ tsp salt

LENTIL RAGÙ
2 Tbsp olive oil
½ cup Harissa, page 211
2½ cups passata
1 cup red lentils
3 cups vegetable stock
2 tsp salt

TO SERVE
1½ lb ditali pasta
2 Tbsp butter
3 cups Egyptian Rice, page 212
1 cup Dakka, page 214

To make the caramelized onions, heat a large frying pan over medium heat. Melt the butter and olive oil, then add the onions and season with salt. Cook on medium-low heat for 1 hour until the natural sugars have released and the onions have reduced considerably. This step can be done 1 to 2 days ahead of serving.

To make the chickpeas, preheat the oven to 425°F and line a baking sheet with parchment paper. Coat the chickpeas in the oil, chili powder, and salt. Roast for 35 to 40 minutes until crispy, shaking the pan occasionally throughout. Keep whole or crush or chop to use as a garnish.

For the lentil ragù, heat the olive oil in a large pot over medium-low heat. Add the harissa, passata, and lentils. Cook for 1 to 2 minutes, then add the stock and the salt. Bring to a boil, then reduce to a simmer. Cook for 30 to 35 minutes until the lentils are tender and the liquid has mostly evaporated. This also can be done 1 to 2 days in advance.

To serve, cook the pasta per the package instructions, undercooking it by 1 minute. Meanwhile, crisp up the caramelized onions in a separate pan with a bit of olive oil.

Add the pasta to the large pot with the lentil ragù and add some of the pasta cooking water, just to cover. Reduce on high until the water evaporates and finishes cooking the pasta, and finish with the butter. To serve, place some of the cooked Egyptian rice on a large plate, add the pasta and ragù, and top with the onions, crispy chickpeas, and a generous dose of the dakka.

LAMB SHOULDER FATTAH WITH ORZO AND CRISPED PITA

SERVES 3–4
PREP TIME: 15 MINUTES
COOK TIME: 3 HOURS
20 MINUTES

It wasn't unusual to see different versions of fattah served over the course of our childhood. My mom's consisted of slow-cooked beef chunks spooned over rice, while her Lebanese friend would always serve a lamb version topped with yogurt and nuts. Either way, the combination of braised meat, earthy spices, and pita topping was always delicious. My version takes inexpensive lamb shoulder chops and turns them into something truly magnificent by braising them in the cardamom and garlic–infused tomato broth. Substitute orzo for the standard rice, add some crunch with the pita, and you're in for a flawless dinner.

◆

PITA
2 cups cubed pita
½ cup butter, melted
Pinch salt

LAMB
2 lb bone-in lamb shoulder chops
Salt and pepper
3 Tbsp olive oil
7 cloves garlic, minced
1 cup beef stock
1 cup passata
⅓ cup tomato paste
1½ tsp ground cumin
1 tsp cinnamon
1 tsp dried mint
½ tsp chili flakes
1 tsp salt
2 bay leaves
6 cardamom pods

ORZO
1¾ cups orzo
¼ cup butter
½ bunch mint, for garnish

For the crisped pita, preheat the oven to 400°F.

In a bowl, toss the cubed pita in the melted butter. Place the cubes on a baking sheet and bake for 10 to 12 minutes until golden brown and crispy. Season with a pinch of salt, and feel free to crush them up with your hands for a finer breadcrumb texture. Store in a resealable container for up to 2 days.

To make the lamb, preheat the oven to 325°F. Pat the lamb shoulder chops dry and season well with salt and pepper.

Heat the olive oil in a Dutch oven on medium-high heat, then sear the chops for 2 to 3 minutes. Flip and sear for another minute, then remove and set aside on a plate. Allow the oil to cool for 1 to 2 minutes, then lower the heat to medium-low. Add the garlic and cook for 1 minute. Deglaze the pot with the stock and increase the heat to medium. Add the passata, tomato paste, cumin, cinnamon, dried mint, chili flakes, salt, bay leaves, and cardamom pods. Return the lamb chops to the pot, cover, and place in the oven. Braise for 2½ to 3 hours until the chops are very tender. This can also be done 1 to 2 days in advance. Reheat in a warm oven before serving.

To make the orzo, boil in salted water for 5 to 6 minutes. Drain, then toss in the butter.

To serve, place the buttery orzo on a platter, then top with the tender lamb shoulder chops. Spoon on some of the braising liquid and top with the crisped pita and some freshly picked mint.

REVERSE-SEARED RIB EYE WITH DAKKA

SERVES 4–6
PREP TIME: 10 MINUTES
COOK TIME: 1 HOUR 35 MINUTES

My dad always ordered steak in a restaurant as "medium" but would follow up his request with a more specific instruction of "but with no pink." I wanted to come up with a steak recipe that would be a true medium, and still be something he could love, even with his prejudice against rosy-hued beef. By slowly rendering the fat in a rib eye, we can keep the meat soft and rich. Top it with the dakka, and you'll have the perfect hit of acidity to cut through the richness of the dish.

◆

1 Tbsp whole coriander seeds

1 Tbsp whole black peppercorns

Four 12 oz rib eye steaks

Salt

3 Tbsp olive oil, for searing

1 cup Dakka, page 214

½ bunch cilantro, picked and roughly chopped

Toast the coriander seeds and peppercorns in a pan over medium heat, tossing regularly, for 2 to 3 minutes, until the aromas are strong. Place the coriander seeds and peppercorns in a spice grinder and coarsely grind them so that you still have some texture. Alternatively, place the spices on a cutting board and use the back of a sauté pan to crush them. Transfer the spices to a small bowl.

Preheat the oven to 225°F and place a wire rack inside a baking sheet. Sprinkle each steak with about ½ teaspoon of the coriander and pepper blend, making sure to season both sides. Place the steaks on the wire rack. Roast for 1¼ to 1½ hours, flipping every 30 minutes, until the steaks have colored but are still a little soft to the touch. Remove the steaks, then season liberally on each side with salt.

In a large pan, heat the olive oil on medium-high heat. Wait for the oil to ripple and the pan to become very hot. Sear the steaks for 30 seconds on one side, then flip and sear for another 30 seconds. Remove the meat, then allow to rest for 5 to 10 minutes. Slice the steak, spoon on the dakka and garnish with the cilantro leaves.

CHICKEN SHARKASEYA WITH WALNUT SAUCE AND CRACKLING

SERVES 4

PREP TIME: 45 MINUTES, PLUS
30 MINUTES FOR SOAKING

COOK TIME: 50 MINUTES

I had never heard of this dish until I told my dear friend Tarek about this book. He insisted I do a version of sharkaseya, which is a poached chicken dish served with a simple walnut sauce. My mom confirmed how significant this dish was: during her childhood, it was reserved for special occasions because nuts were so expensive in those days. My version is moist and tremendously rich from the butter poaching, and the crispy crackling on top offers both texture and a striking presentation.

◆

WALNUT SAUCE

2 slices white bread, cubed, crusts removed

1 cup milk

1½ cups walnuts, divided

1 Tbsp olive oil

1 clove garlic, minced

½ white onion, minced

1 tsp cinnamon

½ tsp nutmeg

1 cup chicken stock

½ tsp salt

½ tsp sugar

CHICKEN

Four 10 oz chicken breasts, bone removed and skin reserved

Salt

1 cup chicken stock

1 lb butter, cubed and chilled

1 tsp xanthan gum (optional, see note)

3 cloves garlic, smashed

1 cinnamon stick

1 bay leaf

To make the walnut sauce, soak the bread in the milk for 30 minutes.

In a dry frying pan over medium heat, toast the walnuts until fragrant, about 3 minutes.

In a saucepan over low heat, heat the olive oil and sweat the garlic and onion for 8 to 10 minutes, until translucent. Add the cinnamon and nutmeg and lightly toast for an additional minute.

Transfer the onion mixture to a blender, with 1 cup of the walnuts, the softened bread and milk, and the stock, salt, and sugar. Blend until very smooth, then strain, discarding any solids.

To make the chicken, preheat the oven to 400°F and line a baking sheet with parchment paper. Place the reserved chicken skins on the baking sheet and cook for 30 to 35 minutes until golden brown and very crispy. Season with salt.

Bring the stock to a simmer in a large saucepan set over medium-low heat. Slowly add the cold butter in stages, whisking constantly. Add the butter gradually and keep it moving to keep it emulsified, and to prevent it from simply melting. You can add the xanthan gum at this point but it's not absolutely necessary. Add the garlic, cinnamon stick, and bay leaf. Then, place the chicken in the liquid. Reduce to low heat and cover. Gently poach for 25 to 30 minutes until the chicken is cooked through but still very tender and moist.

NOTE: You can find xanthan gum more regularly in the grocery store these days; it's often used to stabilize emulsions like this one.

Finely chop the remaining ½ cup of walnuts. Remove the chicken and season with a pinch of salt on each breast before cutting into ½-inch slices. Serve the sliced chicken with a dollop of the walnut sauce, chopped walnuts, and a piece of seasoned skin on top.

MIXED MUSHROOM AND RICE LOAF WITH CHANTERELLE CREAM

SERVES 6–8

PREP TIME: 30 MINUTES, PLUS
4 HOURS FOR SETTING

COOK TIME: 1 HOUR 45 MINUTES

One of the unexpected pleasures of writing this book was discovering unknown family recipes. When digging for ideas, my mom and her sister remembered this baked loaf that my teta would make. She would layer rice with spiced ground meat in a loaf pan, repeating the process to form multiple layers. I wanted to create a similar idea, but chose to use mushrooms instead of the meat. It's important to have tasty vegetarian dishes in your repertoire, and I promise, once you season, cook, then pulse the mushrooms you'll be able to fool even the most avid carnivore. Serve with wilted spinach and top it off with the chanterelle cream for a rich finish.

◆

MUSHROOM AND RICE LOAF

2 cups basmati rice

4 cups vegetable stock

1 tsp salt

6 eggs, beaten, divided

10 oz oyster mushrooms, torn

14 oz portobello mushroom tops
(about 3), roughly chopped

20 oz cremini mushrooms,
roughly chopped

4 Tbsp olive oil, divided

3 shallots, minced

3 cloves garlic, minced

½ tsp allspice

½ tsp cinnamon

½ tsp fenugreek

½ tsp mustard powder

2 Tbsp fresh thyme, chopped

1½ tsp salt

1 cup cashews, finely chopped

1 Tbsp butter

To make the mushroom and rice loaf, first wash off the starch. Place the rice in a strainer and run under cold water, then transfer to a bowl of cold water. Allow the rice to sit for a few minutes. Repeat this process 3 to 4 times until the water is clear and no longer foggy from the starch— this will take 20 to 25 minutes in total.

Place the rinsed rice in a pot with the stock and the salt. Bring to a boil, then cover, reduce the heat, and simmer on medium-low for 18 to 20 minutes. Turn off the heat and let stand for 5 minutes. Remove the lid and fluff the rice with a fork. Wait for the rice to cool completely.

Blitz the oyster, portobello, and cremini mushrooms in a food processor, working in batches, until they are finely ground but not pureed.

Heat 3 tablespoons of the olive oil in a large frying pan over medium-low heat and sweat the shallots and garlic for 3 to 4 minutes, stirring regularly. Add the mushrooms, allspice, cinnamon, fenugreek, mustard powder, thyme, and salt, then increase the heat to medium-high. Cook the mushroom mixture, stirring regularly, until the whole batch shrinks by about half. The water will cook out of the mushrooms, and the flavor will intensify, so don't rush this step! Allow the mixture to cool completely.

Preheat the oven to 350°F. When the rice mixture has cooled, mix in two-thirds of the beaten eggs. When the mushroom mixture has cooled, mix in the chopped cashews and the remaining beaten eggs.

continued on p. 166

CHANTERELLE CREAM

3 cups vegetable stock

1½ oz dried chanterelle
    mushrooms

½ cup cream

Salt

WILTED SPINACH

¼ cup olive oil

3 shallots, minced

3 cloves garlic, minced

15 oz spinach

Grease a 5-by-9-inch loaf pan or line it with parchment paper. Place a layer of the rice mixture, about ¾ inch thick, in the bottom of the pan. Then, top it with a ¾-inch layer of the mushroom mixture. Repeat the process until there are 3 layers of each. Cover the loaf with aluminum foil and bake for 60 to 70 minutes, until set. Remove from the oven and allow to cool completely. Store in the fridge for at least 4 hours or overnight to continue to set.

To make the chanterelle cream, warm the stock slightly in a pot over low heat, and place the chanterelles inside to rehydrate. Let the chanterelles sit in the warm stock for at least 20 minutes.

Remove and reserve the mushrooms and pour the stock through a fine-mesh sieve, discarding any dirt from the mushrooms. Pour the clear stock back into the pot and reduce by half over high heat. Then lower the heat and swirl in the cream and a pinch of salt to taste. Keep warm.

Preheat the oven to 350°F. Cut the cooled mushroom and rice loaf into slices about 1½ inches thick.

Place a large frying pan over medium-high heat and add the remaining tablespoon of olive oil and the butter. Sear each slice for 1 to 2 minutes, until you achieve a nice golden crust. Flip each slice over then place on a baking sheet. I like to sear only the top side, so I get the juxtaposition of a crunchy top and soft rice on the bottom. Place the baking sheet in the oven for 10 minutes to heat the slices through.

To make the wilted spinach, heat the olive oil in a separate pan set over medium-low heat. Sweat the shallots and garlic for 2 minutes. Add the spinach and increase the heat to medium-high. Stir the spinach constantly for 1 to 2 minutes, until it has wilted. Remove from the heat and stir in the reserved, rehydrated chanterelles and season with a pinch of salt.

To serve, place some of the spinach and chanterelles on the bottom of each plate. Top with a slice of the mushroom and rice loaf, then generously spoon on some of the chanterelle cream sauce.

MACARONA BÉCHAMEL WITH VEAL RAGÙ

SERVES 4–6

PREP TIME: 30 MINUTES, PLUS
30 MINUTES CHILLING

COOK TIME: 45 MINUTES

My lifelong love affair with pasta has only grown throughout my professional career, so I wanted to put a spin on a dish that every Egyptian kid ate growing up. Usually, pasta is baked with the meat and béchamel and then portioned out into giant squares. As always, I've kept the flavors authentic while throwing in a few tricks and techniques to make the dish a bit more interesting. I always demanded a crispy corner piece as a kid, so searing the stuffed pasta to get that golden crunch in every bite is an homage to my childhood preference. Truthfully, my mother will probably think this recipe is pretty crazy—until she tries it.

◆

MEAT FILLING

3 Tbsp olive oil

1 white onion, minced

3 cloves garlic, minced

1 lb ground veal

1½ tsp cinnamon

1 tsp ground coriander

1 tsp paprika

¼ tsp chili powder

1 tsp salt

2 Tbsp tomato paste

1 cup beef stock

PASTA

8 oz cannelloni tubes (about 24)

BÉCHAMEL SAUCE

3 Tbsp butter

3 Tbsp flour

2 cups milk

Pinch salt

2 Tbsp lemon juice

Start by making the meat filling. Heat the olive oil in a saucepan set over medium-low heat, and sweat the onion and garlic for 4 to 5 minutes. Add the ground veal, cinnamon, coriander, paprika, chili powder, and salt and increase to medium-high heat for 1 minute, stirring regularly. Add the tomato paste and stock, then bring to a boil. Reduce, then cook on medium heat for 6 to 8 minutes. Be sure to break up the pieces of meat, and stir regularly until almost all of the liquid is gone.

Transfer the meat to your food processor and pulse a few times until the consistency is a bit finer, but not pureed. Allow the meat mixture to cool completely.

To make the pasta, bring a large pot of salted water to a boil and prepare an ice bath. Cook the cannelloni tubes in the boiling water for 4 to 5 minutes, then immediately transfer to a bowl of ice water to halt the cooking process. The pasta should be fairly al dente at this point, as it will cook more later on in the recipe.

Now make your béchamel sauce. Melt the butter in a pot set over medium-low heat, then stir in the flour with a wooden spoon, ensuring no lumps are forming on the bottom or sides of the pot. Cook for 1 to 2 minutes, then add the milk. Bring to a boil, whisking constantly, and cook for 2 to 3 minutes until the sauce is slightly thickened. Season with a pinch of salt and a squeeze of fresh lemon juice.

continued on p. 168

TO SERVE

3 Tbsp butter

1 cup grated pecorino Romano

½ bunch chives, finely chopped

When the pasta and the meat are both chilled, begin the process of stuffing each tube with the veal mixture. Spoon in some of the meat then press down on the pasta to spread it out. Repeat to fill all of the tubes.

Chill the stuffed cannelloni in the fridge, uncovered, for 30 minutes as this will give you a great sear for the next step. If you like, you can make the recipe up to this step and continue cooking the following day. Just be sure to cover the pasta shells well with plastic wrap before storing.

To serve, preheat the oven to 350°F and line a baking sheet with parchment paper.

Heat the butter in a large pan set over medium heat, then add the filled pasta. Sear the pasta for 1 to 2 minutes, until deep golden brown, then remove.

Place the seared pasta on the baking sheet and top each piece with some of the béchamel sauce. Cover with the pecorino cheese, then bake for 10 minutes to heat through. Finally, set the oven to broil, and cook for an additional minute, watching carefully to make sure the shells don't burn. Remove from the oven and garnish with fresh chives.

GRILLED CALAMARI WITH TOMATO JAM

SERVES 4–6

PREP TIME: 15 MINUTES, PLUS
2 HOURS FOR SEASONING

COOK TIME: 2 HOURS 30 MINUTES
FOR JAM, 5 MINUTES FOR
CALAMARI

Middle Eastern calamari is often stewed with tomatoes and herbs, but coastal cities will serve it grilled with fresh cilantro, lemon, and tomatoes, which is the way I prefer it. This version makes a big batch of tomato jam—much more than you need for this particular recipe—but it will keep in the fridge for up to 10 days, goes well with eggs, and can also be frozen.

◆

TOMATO JAM

3 Tbsp olive oil

1 red onion, minced

8 cloves garlic, minced

2 Tbsp fresh ginger, minced

Two 26 oz cans peeled tomatoes

3 Tbsp brown sugar

½ cup molasses

⅓ cup red wine vinegar

½ tsp chili flakes

¾ tsp salt

GRILLED CALAMARI

2 lb squid, cleaned

2 tsp ground coriander

2 tsp black pepper

1 tsp turmeric

1 tsp smoked paprika

1 tsp onion powder

1 tsp garlic powder

¼ cup olive oil

1 white onion, sliced

½ bunch cilantro, finely chopped,
    plus extra for garnish

TO SERVE

2 lemons, for squeezing

For the tomato jam, heat the olive oil in a pot set over medium-low heat. Add the onion, garlic, and ginger. Reduce the heat to low and sweat for 10 to 12 minutes. Add the canned tomatoes, brown sugar, molasses, vinegar, chili flakes, and salt. Bring to a boil, then reduce to a simmer and cook for about 2½ hours, until the jam appears darker and has thickened. Store leftovers in a resealable plastic container which will keep in the fridge for up to 10 days.

For the calamari, slice some of the squid into rings, some into scored squares, which will curl up into a nice shape, and keep some pieces whole so that you can stuff some tomato jam inside.

In a large bowl, combine the coriander, black pepper, turmeric, paprika, onion powder, and garlic powder. Add the olive oil and whisk to combine. Add the onion and cilantro, followed by the calamari. Toss to coat and refrigerate for 2 hours.

Bring the calamari to room temperature before grilling. If you are stuffing some pieces with jam, make sure the jam is cool.

Rub your barbecue or grill pan with some oil, heat to high, then place the calamari and onions on top, only grilling for 1 to 3 minutes, depending on the size of the piece—the rings will cook quickly, while the stuffed tubes take a bit longer. Turn the calamari halfway through the cooking process. Remove from the grill and drizzle with fresh lemon juice, along with a generous pinch of salt.

Serve with the tomato jam, extra cilantro leaves, and some lemons for squeezing.

BLACK LIME RACK OF LAMB
WITH CURED OLIVE PAN SAUCE

SERVES 2–3
PREP TIME: 10 MINUTES, PLUS
1 HOUR FOR SEASONING
COOK TIME: 20–25 MINUTES

A roasted rack of lamb is a thing of beauty, and most definitely a dish you need in your repertoire. This recipe, complete with the black lime powder, is a showstopper. Find black limes in any Middle Eastern grocery store and grind them up into a "secret weapon" spice. It's tangy, citrusy, and a bit bitter, so it offers a ton of depth and an interesting hit on the palate that few will recognize right away, but all will salivate over.

◆

LAMB
1 tsp black lime powder, plus extra
   for garnish (see note)
½ tsp paprika
½ tsp cinnamon
1⅓ lb rack of lamb
2 Tbsp olive oil

CURED OLIVE SAUCE
1 cup beef stock
¼ cup cured black olives, pitted
2 Tbsp cold butter, cubed

TO SERVE
½ cup Greek yogurt

◆

NOTE: To make black lime powder, take a few black limes, place them in a spice grinder, then pulse well to form a fine powder. Transfer to a resealable plastic container, as this powder keeps for up to 1 month.

To prepare the lamb, mix the black lime powder, paprika, and cinnamon together, then rub the mixture into the meat on all sides and refrigerate for 1 hour. When you're about 30 minutes away from being ready to cook, bring the lamb out of the fridge to let it come to room temperature (a cardinal mistake is to start cooking meat that's stone cold from the fridge!). Season the lamb very lightly with salt—the cured olives in the sauce are quite salty and will carry the heavy lifting in this dish.

Preheat the oven to 400°F. Heat the olive oil in an ovenproof skillet over medium-high heat. Sear the lamb for 2 minutes without moving it, then flip and sear on the other sides, another minute or two in total. Transfer the skillet to the oven and roast for 18 to 19 minutes (adjusting this roasting time according to size).

Remove the lamb from the oven and take out of the skillet, allowing to rest for at least 10 minutes on a cutting board. I prefer my lamb to be pink but not too rare. For me, a great rule of thumb is to roast the lamb for about 14 minutes per pound after searing.

To make the olive sauce, drain the skillet of excess oil, then add the stock and the olives. Heat on high and reduce the stock for 4 to 5 minutes. Once reduced by about half, turn off the heat and swirl in the cold butter, allowing it to emulsify into a sauce. Keep moving the pan as you incorporate the butter or it may split and the sauce will become greasy. Even without salt, you may feel that the sauce has a touch too much saltiness from the olives, but remember you've barely seasoned the lamb, so it will all work together.

Serve the lamb with the sauce and some thick yogurt, and top the whole dish with another dash of the black lime powder.

HARISSA CHICKEN THIGHS WITH SAFFRON ISRAELI COUSCOUS

SERVES 6

PREP TIME: 15 MINUTES, PLUS AT LEAST 2 HOURS FOR MARINATING

COOK TIME: 35 MINUTES

Over the past few years, the number-one question people have asked me over and over again is how they can get out of their dinner rut at home. Chicken thighs are one of those basic items that are perfect for a weeknight meal—they're affordable, deliciously fatty, and hard to over-cook. This harissa marinade makes an everyday cut of meat more inter-esting by introducing heat, sweetness, and a bold color. Work this meal into your rotation, and you'll literally spice up the whole week.

◆

HARISSA CHICKEN

1 cup Harissa, page 211

¼ cup olive oil

2 cloves garlic, minced

2 Tbsp brown sugar

2 lb chicken thighs, bone in and skin on

Salt

3 Tbsp olive oil

1 cup chicken stock

SAFFRON ISRAELI COUSCOUS

¼ cup olive oil

2 cups Israeli couscous

Pinch salt

¼ cup Saffron Butter, page 212

To make the harissa chicken, in a large mixing bowl, combine the harissa, olive oil, garlic, brown sugar, and ¼ cup water. Add the chicken, cover with plastic wrap and refrigerate for at least 2 hours, or even marinate overnight.

Bring the chicken to room temperature and preheat the oven to 400°F. Reserve the excess marinade, but pat the chicken dry to help with the sear. Season with salt.

Heat the olive oil in a large ovenproof skillet over medium-high heat. Add the chicken, skin side down, and sear for 1 to 2 minutes. Flip over and transfer to a plate or sheet pan. Work in batches if necessary, to avoid overcrowding the pan.

Deglaze the pan with the chicken stock, scraping up any brown bits with a wooden spoon. Add the reserved marinade and bring to a boil. Add the chicken back to the pan, in one layer, and roast in the oven for about 35 minutes or until the internal temperature is 165°F.

To make the saffron Israeli couscous, heat the olive oil in a large skillet set over medium-high heat. Add the couscous and toast for 1 to 2 min-utes, allowing the couscous to brown and achieve a nutty, more com-plex flavor. Cover with 5 cups water and salt, then bring to a boil. Reduce to a simmer and cook for 15 to 16 minutes, or until all of the liquid has been absorbed and the couscous is al dente. Finish by stirring in the saffron butter and an additional pinch of salt if needed.

Serve each plate with some couscous on the bottom, topped with a chicken thigh and some of the remaining sauce.

SWEETS
TO FINISH

AUNT SUSIE'S FAMOUS STAR COOKIES

MAKES 24 SANDWICH COOKIES
PREP TIME: 1 HOUR
COOK TIME: 15 MINUTES

Some of my best Christmas memories center on the long trek to Aunt Susie's house in Sherbrooke, Quebec, after which my parents would be too exhausted from the snowy eight-hour drive to care how many cookies I ate before and after dinner. Ironically, because Aunt Susie is one tough cookie herself, her signature treat is quite the opposite.

◆

¾ lb butter, room temperature

1 cup sugar

3 eggs

1 tsp vanilla extract

6 cups all-purpose flour

2 tsp cinnamon

1 tsp baking powder

1 tsp salt

1½ cups apricot jam, for filling

¼ cup powdered sugar, for dusting

Preheat the oven to 350°F and line a baking sheet with parchment paper. Place the butter in the bowl of a stand mixer and add the sugar. Cream the butter and sugar together for several minutes until light and fluffy. With the mixer on, add one egg at a time followed by the vanilla extract.

In a separate bowl, mix the flour, cinnamon, baking powder, and salt.

Add the dry mix to the creamed butter and egg in the mixer bowl. Mix again on low just to combine and try to avoid overmixing.

Divide the dough into 4 even pieces, wrap tightly with plastic, and refrigerate for a few minutes to cool down.

Once the dough has cooled, dust your work surface with a touch of flour. Roll out the first piece of dough until it's very thin, about ¹⁄₁₆ inch. This is a sandwich cookie, so we want both layers to be thin.

Using a cookie cutter, cut out 12 circles and carefully place them on the baking sheet, at least 1 inch apart (you may need two baking sheets, or to bake the cookies in batches). Repeat with the other pieces of dough. For half of the circles, take a small star-shaped cookie cutter (or any other shape that you have on hand) and cut out a little star in the middle of the pieces that will make the top halves of the sandwich. Bake the cookies for 12 to 15 minutes, rotating at the halfway point and being mindful to not allow much color. Remove from the oven and allow to cool completely.

Dollop about 1 tablespoon of apricot jam on the bottom half of the sandwich circle (the cookies that don't have a cut-out star). Then dust some powdered sugar on the top halves (the circles that do have a cut-out) and place on top of the jam-filled bottoms.

CLASSIC KONAFA WITH WINE AND CHERRY COMPOTE

SERVES 10
PREP TIME: 25 MINUTES
COOK TIME: 40 MINUTES

Sometimes you don't need to mess with a classic. Almost every Middle Eastern culture has a version of this warm and golden dessert, and it's pretty perfect just as it is. As a kid, one of my favorite foods was cheesecake (maybe I was watching too many episodes of *The Golden Girls*) and I loved the cream cheese and fruit elements of this beautiful dessert as well. This crispy and creamy sweet treat brings me back to countless family dinner parties.

◆

FILLING

4 oz brick-style cream cheese, softened

1 cup whipping cream

1 cup milk

⅓ cup sugar

1 Tbsp vanilla bean paste, or 1 tsp vanilla extract

¼ cup cornstarch

2 Tbsp maraschino liqueur

Pinch salt

SYRUP

½ cup sugar

1 Tbsp maraschino liqueur

PHYLLO CRUST

1 lb shredded phyllo dough, thawed

1 cup butter, melted

WINE AND CHERRY COMPOTE

2 cups cherries, pitted

1 cup Cabernet Sauvignon

¼ cup brown sugar

1 tsp cinnamon

½ cup pistachios, finely chopped

Start by making the cream cheese filling. In a pot set over medium heat, combine the cream cheese, cream, milk, sugar, and vanilla bean paste. Melt the ingredients together for 1 to 2 minutes.

In a small bowl, make a slurry with your cornstarch by mixing it with equal parts cold water, then add it to the mixture and bring to a boil to activate the thickening properties, whisking constantly. Cook on high heat for 1 to 2 minutes until the mixture becomes thick. Whisk in the maraschino liqueur and salt. Allow to cool completely.

To make the syrup, combine the sugar, maraschino liqueur, and ½ cup water in a pot over high heat. Bring to a boil to fully dissolve the sugar, then allow to cool completely.

To make the phyllo crust, preheat the oven to 375°F and generously grease the bottom and the sides of a 9-inch pie tin with butter.

Cut the shredded phyllo dough into small pieces and place them in a large mixing bowl. Pour the melted butter on top, then evenly toss the phyllo pieces. Place about 3 cups of the shredded phyllo dough into the pie tin. Press down on the phyllo using your hands or the bottom of a measuring cup to make a compact crust. Next, place the cooled cream cheese filling on top and spread evenly with a spatula. Top with another 2 cups of shredded phyllo and gently press down. Bake for 30 minutes.

To make the wine and cherry compote, combine the cherries, red wine, brown sugar, and cinnamon in a pot and bring to a boil. Reduce to a simmer and cook for 8 to 10 minutes until thickened.

Remove the konafa from the oven and immediately pour the cold maraschino syrup overtop. Allow to sit for 10 to 15 minutes, then invert onto a serving platter, exposing the golden brown bottom. To serve, spoon on the wine and cherry compote and sprinkle on some finely chopped pistachios. Cut into slices and enjoy.

SOURDOUGH OM ALI BREAD PUDDING WITH COCONUT SAUCE

SERVES 6
PREP TIME: 40 MINUTES
COOK TIME: 35 MINUTES

The "bread" in Egyptian bread pudding is often puff pastry that's been cooked, cubed, and soaked. However, I find that a high-quality sourdough soaks up the tasty liquid a bit better. Serve with the warm coconut sauce and you have the best comfort food dessert.

◆

30 dates
3 egg yolks
1 whole egg
¾ cup whipping cream
½ cup milk
½ cup sweetened condensed milk
¼ cup brown sugar
2 tsp cinnamon
About 4 cups cubed sourdough bread
½ cup dried unsweetened coconut
½ cup finely chopped walnuts
½ cup raisins
½ tsp salt

COCONUT SAUCE
One 13 oz can coconut milk
⅓ cup sweetened condensed milk
¼ cup brown sugar
½ tsp cinnamon
Pinch salt

Soak the dates in warm water for at least 20 minutes.

In a large mixing bowl, whisk together the egg yolks, egg, cream, milk, and sweetened condensed milk. Add the brown sugar and cinnamon and whisk well to incorporate. Add the bread, coconut, walnuts, raisins, and salt. Using a spatula, gently toss all of the ingredients together. Allow the bread to soak for 30 minutes; this is a crucial step in a great bread pudding!

Preheat the oven to 350°F.

Drain the dates, reserving the soaking liquid. Add the dates to a food processor along with ½ cup of the liquid, and blend until very smooth. Add the pureed dates to the bread pudding and fold in.

Divide the bread pudding into 6 ramekins or one large serving dish and bake for 30 to 35 minutes (about 45 minutes if baking in a single dish).

To make the coconut sauce, combine the coconut milk, sweetened condensed milk, brown sugar, cinnamon, and salt in a pot over medium-high heat and bring to a boil. Reduce the heat to low and simmer for 10 to 12 minutes until slightly thickened. The sauce should coat the back of a spoon and hold the shape of a line when you run your finger through it.

Serve the bread pudding warm with the coconut sauce.

CHEWY CAROB MOLASSES COOKIES

SERVES 4–6
PREP TIME: 15 MINUTES
COOK TIME: 10 MINUTES

It's about time that carob molasses got a little recognition. Derived from the pods of the carob tree, this molasses has more character and depth than its sugarcane counterpart. With notes of chocolate, caramel, and even a subtle hint of bitterness, this Middle Eastern staple should be stocked in your pantry. Try experimenting with it in other baking and even your next batch of barbecue sauce.

◆

½ cup butter, softened
⅓ cup granulated sugar
¼ cup brown sugar
1 egg
⅓ cup carob molasses
2 cups all-purpose flour
2 tsp baking powder
½ tsp salt
1½ tsp cinnamon
½ tsp ginger
¼ tsp nutmeg
¼ cup turbinado sugar

Preheat the oven to 350°F and line a baking sheet with parchment paper.

Place the butter, granulated sugar, and brown sugar in a large mixing bowl. With a handheld mixer (or even whisk by hand if you need the workout), cream the butter and sugar together, whisking for several minutes until pale and fluffy. Add the egg, whisk to combine, then add the molasses and mix well.

In a separate bowl, combine the flour, baking powder, salt, cinnamon, ginger, and nutmeg. Whisk well to combine, then add to the bowl of wet ingredients. Fold in evenly, making sure not to overmix.

Take approximately ¼ cup of the batter to form each cookie. Roll into a little ball in your hands, then roll in the turbinado sugar. Place the cookie on the baking sheet and gently flatten out to form a nice, circular cookie. Bake the cookies for 9 to 10 minutes or until slightly expanded, then let them cool slightly to firm up (they will seem a bit soft at first).

PISTACHIO TART WITH COOKIE CRUST, WILD BLUEBERRIES, AND OLIVE OIL

SERVES 8–10

PREP TIME: 20 MINUTES, PLUS 3 HOURS FOR COOLING

COOK TIME: 1 HOUR 10 MINUTES

I loved working in hyper-busy New York City kitchens, but was equally happy in those rare moments when things slowed down. One night, as the end of service was nearing at Lupa, Chef Cruz gave me a spoonful of pistachio gelato that he had made. It was delicious. He then gave me another spoonful of the same gelato, but topped it with a touch of high-quality olive oil and a pinch of salt. Immediately the flavor graduated to outrageously mind-blowing. This creamy tart captures that experience, with the blueberries adding a fruity touch.

◆

TART FILLING

5 egg yolks

½ cup sugar

1 Tbsp vanilla paste, or 1 tsp vanilla extract

2 cups milk

3 Tbsp cornstarch

½ cup Pistachio Butter, page 221

COOKIE CRUST

23 digestive cookies

¼ cup + 2 Tbsp sugar

¼ cup + 2 Tbsp butter, melted

For the tart filling, whisk the egg yolks and sugar together in a large mixing bowl by hand for 3 to 4 minutes. The mixture will take on a pale-yellow color and thicken to the point where you can drizzle a figure eight. Add the vanilla paste and mix well.

In a medium pot, bring the milk to a gentle simmer. Slowly whisk some warm milk into the creamed yolk and sugar mixture. Add the rest of the milk in a few installments while whisking continuously. Once all the milk has been added, return the entire mixture to the pot.

In a separate small bowl, make a slurry by whisking the cornstarch with an equal amount of cold water.

Add the cornstarch slurry to the mixture in the pot and whisk well to combine. Bring to a boil while whisking continuously to activate the cornstarch. Once the mixture has thickened, remove from the heat. Strain into a clean bowl (to capture any egg bits that may have scrambled), then stir in the pistachio butter. Allow to cool completely.

Preheat the oven to 375°F.

To make the cookie crust, place the cookies in the bowl of a food processor. Blitz the cookies until they become fine crumbs; you should have about 3 cups.

continued on p. 188

TOPPING
1½ cups wild blueberries
⅓ cup good-quality olive oil
⅓ cup pistachios, finely ground
Pinch salt

Place the crumbs in a mixing bowl, then mix in the sugar and melted butter. The consistency should feel like wet sand on the beach (a surprisingly depressing image, as I developed this recipe during a freezing Canadian winter).

Place the crumbs in the bottom of an 11-inch fluted tart pan, making sure to press the crumbs up the sides to make a compact crust. You can also make individual tarts in mini tart shells, with ¼ cup of crumbs per shell, using the bottom of a measuring cup to compact the crust. Bake in the oven for 15 minutes, then remove and allow to cool.

Reduce the oven temperature to 350°F. Fill the cooled tart shell with the cooled filling and bake for 45 minutes (30 minutes for the mini tart size). Remove and allow to cool completely. Place in the fridge for at least 4 hours, up to overnight to firm up.

When ready to serve, top with a generous amount of blueberries, a drizzle of olive oil, the chopped pistachios, and a pinch of salt.

STUFFED ARABIC PANCAKES
WITH MAPLE-GLAZED APPLES

SERVES 6–8
PREP TIME: 40 MINUTES
COOK TIME: 50 MINUTES

Years ago, my wife, Mila, and I took a romantic trip to Montreal and enjoyed the city's vibrant dining scene. We spent one memorable night in one of Old Montreal's hippest restaurants—the music was pumping, the food was incredible, and I'm pretty sure the bartender drank more than he served. It was all magical. Dessert that evening was . . . pancakes. I couldn't believe how this little stack of pancakes, drizzled with real Quebec maple syrup, could be such a perfect way to end a meal. Think of this recipe as more than just a brunch staple and try ending your next dinner party with these gems. Arabic pancakes differ from North American ones in that the batter has a bit of yeast, along with semolina flour for a distinctive taste.

◆

STUFFED ARABIC PANCAKES

½ tsp active dry yeast

1 cup semolina flour

½ cup all-purpose flour

1 Tbsp sugar

1 tsp baking powder

¼ tsp salt

1½ cups buttermilk

2 Tbsp butter, melted, plus more for frying

Vegetable oil, for shallow frying

Powdered sugar, for dusting

MAPLE-GLAZED APPLES

1 lb Gala apples, peeled

2 Tbsp butter

1 tsp cinnamon

¼ cup maple syrup

MASCARPONE FILLING

1½ cups mascarpone

3 Tbsp sugar

1 Tbsp vanilla bean paste, or 1 tsp vanilla extract

Pinch salt

Start the pancakes by placing ½ cup of warm water in a bowl, and sprinkling on the yeast to bloom. Let sit for 10 minutes, until the water becomes foggy from the activated yeast.

In a large bowl, combine the semolina flour, all-purpose flour, sugar, baking powder, and salt and whisk well. Add the buttermilk and melted butter. Add the yeast and mix. Add another 2 to 3 tablespoons of water if needed to reach the desired consistency. You're looking for a batter that's somewhere between a pancake and crepe—not too thick, but not watery thin either. Allow the batter to rest for 10 to 15 minutes.

To make the glazed apples, cut the apples into 1-inch-thick pieces.

Place the apples in a large frying pan and add the butter, cinnamon, maple syrup, and 1½ cups water. Bring to a boil, then reduce to a low simmer for 20 to 22 minutes. The apples should be nice and tender, and the water and maple should reduce to a delicious syrup.

To make the filling, combine the mascarpone, sugar, vanilla, and salt. Whisk well, then set in the fridge.

continued on p. 190

Line a baking sheet with parchment paper. Melt 1 to 2 tablespoons of butter in a small nonstick pan set over medium-low heat. Turn the heat to low and add a small ladleful (about 2 to 3 tablespoons) of pancake batter. Swirl the pan around to make a circle, then cook for 1 minute. The pancake is done when a series of bubbles begins to form on the top. Unlike a traditional pancake, don't flip it at this point!

Transfer the pancake to the lined baking sheet and cover with a moist kitchen towel to prevent it drying out. Repeat until all the pancakes have been cooked, about 16 to 18 pancakes total. Allow to cool.

Place 1 tablespoon of the mascarpone filling in the middle of a pancake. Wet the edges of the pancake by dipping your finger in water (this helps to seal them well) then enclose each one. Squeeze the edges well to seal them tightly, and press along the filling to remove any air bubbles. Keep them under the moist kitchen towel as you work. If serving later, this can be done a few hours in advance, as long as they are well covered.

To finish, heat the vegetable oil in a large skillet over medium heat. Add the stuffed pancakes, working in batches, and crisp on all sides, 1 to 2 minutes total. Transfer to a plate lined with paper towel and repeat until all of the pancakes are golden brown and crispy. Serve with the maple-glazed apples and a little dusting of powdered sugar!

BROWN BUTTER AND COCONUT BASBOUSA

MAKES 12–18 SMALL CAKES
PREP TIME: 20 MINUTES
COOK TIME: 30–40 MINUTES

This classic Egyptian coconut semolina cake is near and dear to my heart. Firstly, I made this for Mila as a perfect ending to our first date. Also, this was the recipe that I was making on a TV show when I was discovered by the CBC! Browning the butter in this recipe gives a nutty and rich tone, while the yogurt keeps the cake moist and crumbly. Try this recipe at home, and who knows, maybe your life will take an unexpected and pleasant turn too.

◆

1 lb butter
1½ cups unsweetened dried
   coconut
1½ cups sugar
1½ cups plain yogurt
1 Tbsp vanilla extract
2¾ cups semolina flour
3 tsp baking powder
2 tsp salt

COCONUT GLAZE
1 cup whipping cream
½ cup icing sugar
Pinch salt
⅛ tsp coconut extract

ORANGE SYRUP
1 cup orange juice
½ cup sugar

GARNISH
1 cup almonds, toasted and finely
   chopped

◆

NOTE: This recipe will yield about 18 mini muffin–sized cakes. Reduce the baking time to about 25 minutes to account for the smaller size.

Preheat the oven to 350°F and grease a 12-cup muffin tin.

In a small pot over medium heat, start to melt the butter, then add the coconut to toast. Cook together until the coconut is golden brown and the butter is browned and smells nutty, about 5 minutes.

Transfer to a large bowl and stir to cool. Add the sugar and whisk until creamed together evenly and the mixture is aromatic and amber-colored. Add the yogurt and vanilla extract and mix to combine.

In separate bowl, whisk together the semolina flour, baking powder, and salt, then add to the wet ingredients. Mix just to combine. Divide evenly into the muffin tin and bake for 35 to 40 minutes, or until a cake tester inserted into the center comes out clean.

To make the coconut glaze, whisk the cream and icing sugar together just to mix. Add the salt and coconut extract.

To make the orange syrup, combine the orange juice and sugar in a small pot over medium-high heat and reduce for about 5 minutes.

When the cakes come out of the oven, use a pastry brush to mop each cake with syrup to keep it moist, then keep covered until ready to serve.

To serve, warm the cakes in a 325°F oven for a few minutes, then top with the coconut glaze and chopped almonds.

APRICOT MISHMISH

SERVES 10–12

PREP TIME: 45 MINUTES, PLUS
OVERNIGHT TO CHILL

COOK TIME: 30 MINUTES

This mishmish is similar to a panna cotta, one of my go-to dessert recipes. It's soft and creamy, and when topped with chopped pistachios and honey syrup, you've got a stunning dessert that you can make for guests ahead of time and stress-free.

◆

MISHMISH

1 cup dried apricots

4 oz brick-style cream cheese

1½ cups whole milk

1½ cups whipping cream

1 cup plain yogurt

½ cup sugar

1 Tbsp vanilla extract

1 tsp salt

1½ Tbsp gelatin powder

APRICOT AND HONEY SYRUP

1 cup dried apricots, finely diced

½ cup honey

GARNISH

½ cup pistachios, toasted and
   finely ground

To make the mishmish, cover the dried apricots in very hot water to soften. Let sit at least 30 minutes and then drain, discarding the water.

In a blender, combine the softened apricots with the cream cheese, milk, cream, yogurt, sugar, vanilla, and salt. Blend until very smooth.

Take a small amount of the blended mixture and put it in a separate bowl. Sprinkle the gelatin over the small amount, then top with ⅓ cup boiling water. Stir well to bloom the gelatin. Add back to the apricot mixture and blend again to incorporate.

Divide the mixture into silicone molds or into mousse cups and chill in the fridge for at least 4 hours or preferably overnight.

To make the syrup, bring the apricots, honey, and 1 cup water to a boil in a small pot, then gently simmer for 30 minutes. This can be made a few days in advance, but add some hot water to loosen it before serving. You want to have a saucy consistency that you can drizzle around the plate.

To serve, unmold the mishmish onto a plate and garnish with toasted pistachios. Drizzle some apricot and honey syrup on the side and enjoy.

KAHK COOKIES

MAKES 12 COOKIES
PREP TIME: 1 HOUR
COOK TIME: 20 MINUTES

These cookies were a staple at big family events and special holidays. You would see kids running around hopped up, with powdered sugar all over themselves! But make no mistake, even adults will have a hard time not reaching back for seconds and thirds, as these crumbly little cookies are hard to resist. These treats can have a variety of different fillings, but my favorite growing up was always the date flavor.

◆

1 cup dried dates
½ cup melted butter
½ cup milk
1 tsp vanilla extract
2 cups all-purpose flour
½ cup powdered sugar, plus more for dusting
1 Tbsp ground anise
1 Tbsp mahlab (optional, see note)
½ tsp baking powder
½ tsp salt

Cover the dates in very hot water and let sit for 30 minutes, or up to 1 hour. Strain the dates, discarding the water, and blend them in a food processor.

Preheat the oven to 350°F and line a baking sheet with parchment paper.

Combine the melted butter with the milk and vanilla extract.

In a separate bowl, combine the flour, powdered sugar, anise, mahlab, baking powder, and salt.

Pour the butter mixture into the bowl with the dry ingredients. Use a spatula (a bit easier than a whisk for a wetter dough like this) to fold together the ingredients.

Divide the dough into 12 even balls. Make an indent in each ball to make room for 1 teaspoon of date filling. Enclose the filling inside the ball of dough, then flatten into a cookie. You can keep them circular (which is traditional) and score the top with a fork, or use a mold to create a unique shape, as I've done in the photo.

Chill the cookies in the fridge for 15 minutes, then remove and bake on the lined baking sheets for about 20 minutes. Allow to cool completely, then top with a generous dusting of powdered sugar.

◆

NOTE: Mahlab is a special ingredient found in Middle Eastern grocery stores and has beautiful almond and cherry notes. However, if you can't find it, the anise in the recipe provides a similar effect.

STRAWBERRY PASTA FLORA

SERVES 8–10

PREP TIME: 20 MINUTES, PLUS 30 MINUTES RESTING

COOK TIME: 45 MINUTES

When looking for a new dessert idea, my dad enthusiastically said that his mom (my Teta Souna) would always make a jam-filled tart called *pasta flora*. He described a rich crust filled with sweet fruit filling, and I was immediately intrigued. I had so many questions: Did she make it for special occasions? What was her recipe? What does "pasta flora" even mean? Well, my dad has absolutely no idea. He only knows that when she made it, he loved it, so here's my best shot at replicating her magic.

◆

STRAWBERRY FILLING

4 cups sliced frozen strawberries

⅓ cup sugar

1 Tbsp vanilla bean paste, or 1 tsp vanilla extract

½ tsp salt

⅛ tsp white pepper (optional)

3 Tbsp cornstarch

CRUST

1 cup butter, softened

½ cup brown sugar

½ cup granulated sugar

4 egg yolks

1 Tbsp vanilla bean paste, or 1 tsp vanilla extract

1½ cups all-purpose flour

1½ cups semolina flour

1 tsp baking powder

½ tsp salt

1 egg, beaten

TO SERVE

Rosewater Whipped Cream, page 220, for serving

To make the strawberry filling, in a large pot, combine the frozen strawberries with 1 cup of water and the sugar, vanilla, salt, and white pepper. Bring to a boil, then reduce the heat and simmer for about 10 minutes.

In a small bowl, mix the cornstarch with 3 tablespoons of water to create a slurry. Drizzle the cornstarch slurry into the strawberry mixture and bring to a boil again to thicken. Boil for 1 minute, then reduce and simmer for 2 minutes. Allow the strawberry filling to cool completely, then transfer to the fridge to firm up for a few hours. This can be done the day before making the pasta flora.

To make the crust, in a mixing bowl, cream the butter, brown sugar, and sugar for 5 to 6 minutes with a handheld mixer until pale and fluffy. Then, add the yolks, one at a time, followed by the vanilla bean paste.

In a separate bowl, combine the all-purpose flour, semolina flour, baking powder, and salt, and mix well. Add the dry ingredients to the wet, and combine just to bring together. It's better to have small chunks that you can bring together with your hands than to overmix a dough like this.

Take half of the crust mix and press it into the bottom and up the sides of a 9-inch tart pan, preferably one that's nonstick with a removable bottom. Cover with plastic wrap. Bring the other half of the crust dough together and wrap tightly in plastic. Place the wrapped dough and the pressed dough in the fridge to relax for 30 minutes.

Preheat the oven to 350°F. Remove the tart pan from the fridge and spread the strawberry filling evenly along the bottom. Sprinkle some flour on a work surface and roll out the other half of the crust dough to about ⅛ inch thick.

Use a cookie cutter to cut out shapes as desired. I like a flower motif to match the "flora" name. Place the cut-out shapes on top, then brush the crust with some egg wash. Bake for 30 minutes.

To serve, allow the tart to cool completely. Take out of the pan, slice, and serve with rosewater whipped cream.

SWEET AND SAVORY DUKKAH BRITTLE

SERVES 12
PREP TIME: 15 MINUTES
COOK TIME: 10 MINUTES

Every time I entertain, I have a meat and cheese board ready for guests. Aside from trying to be hospitable, this gives me some breathing room when preparing the actual meal—the last thing you want is starving people staring at you while you're trying to cook for a crowd. However, I always replenish the cheese selection at the end of the meal too, as it's a casual way to keep nibbling along with some dessert wine or digestifs. Add this brittle to your cheese board repertoire, and you'll never turn back. It's sweet, spicy, savory, and really interesting along with sharp cheeses and soft bread.

◆

½ cup Dukkah, page 218
2 cups sugar

Line a baking sheet with a silicone baking mat or parchment paper and evenly sprinkle the dukkah overtop.

Combine the sugar and 1 cup water in a saucepan over medium-high heat and begin to caramelize. Swirl the pan from time to time to ensure even cooking and to prevent crystallization on the sides. Cook for 7 to 10 minutes, until the sugar turns an amber color and you can smell a nutty caramel note.

Immediately remove from the heat and pour evenly over the dukkah. You want a nice even layer so that you avoid having spots that are thick chunks of solid sugar. Allow to cool completely, then break off rustic pieces by hand. Store in an airtight container for up to 14 days.

CAST-IRON FETEER WITH WILDFLOWER HONEY AND CINNAMON

SERVES 6

PREP TIME: 20 MINUTES, PLUS
TIME FOR RESTING THE DOUGH

COOK TIME: 20 MINUTES

1 batch Feteer Dough, divided into
   6 balls, page 222

¾ cup melted butter + 3 Tbsp
   butter, divided

¾ cup wildflower honey

2 Tbsp cinnamon

3 tsp vegetable oil

Powdered sugar, for dusting

Vanilla ice cream, for serving

There's no room for error when you're using only honey and cinnamon on a dough of just flour and water. I found after baking these in a hot oven that the results were just OK. But after cooking them in a hot sturdy cast-iron pan, they became molten crunchy little packages of warmth and spice. Cook these up on a fall day for brunch or serve with cold vanilla ice cream at the end of a dinner for an Egyptian à la mode experience.

◆

Make the feteer dough and allow to rest for at least 1 hour. I like to make my dough several hours in advance, or even the day before to allow it to rest in the fridge. A cool dough is a bit easier and more forgiving to work with in this particular recipe.

Divide the dough into 6 pieces. Stretch out each piece of dough with your fingers and hands until it is very thin. Paint each piece with about 2 tablespoons of melted butter. Drizzle on about 2 tablespoons of wildflower honey, and sprinkle on 1 teaspoon of cinnamon with your fingers.

Enclose each feteer by folding from the bottom to the middle and repeating all the way around to create a circular shape, similar to how you would make a galette. Don't worry, the shape doesn't have to be perfect at all!

Heat some of the butter and oil in a cast-iron skillet set over medium heat. Once melted, add a feteer, folded side up, and cook for 2 to 3 minutes until the bottom becomes golden brown. Flip and reduce the heat to medium-low. Cook for another 2 to 3 minutes until cooked through. If you find that the center of the feteer has thicker pieces of dough (this can happen, considering each side has been folded into the center) you can cut these out with a circular cookie cutter. Repeat with the remaining feteers.

Dust the feteers with a touch of powdered sugar and serve with vanilla ice cream.

ASHTA ICE CREAM WITH ROASTED FIGS AND GRAPE VINEGAR REDUCTION

SERVES 8

PREP TIME: 30 MINUTES, PLUS TIME FOR SETTING

COOK TIME: 2 HOURS 45 MINUTES

Ashta, or Middle Eastern double cream, combines with brown sugar to make a simple ice cream with a complex caramel-like flavor. Just blend the ingredients together (unlike an egg-based ice cream, it doesn't need to be cooked first), then thicken and stabilize the mixture with the secret ingredient—xanthan gum. Top it with other quintessential Middle Eastern ingredients (slow-roasted figs and a reduction made from Lebanese grape vinegar), and you've got a unique ending to any meal.

◆

ASHTA ICE CREAM

1½ cups milk

1 cup whipping cream

⅓ cup ashta

⅓ cup brown sugar

1 Tbsp vanilla bean paste, or 1 tsp vanilla extract

¾ tsp salt

¼ tsp xanthan gum (see note)

ROASTED FIGS

17 oz dried figs

⅓ cup butter, melted

¼ cup brown sugar

GRAPE VINEGAR REDUCTION

2 cups grape vinegar, or good-quality balsamic vinegar

¼ cup sugar

To make the ice cream, combine the milk, cream, ashta, brown sugar, vanilla, and salt in a blender. Blend on low, just to incorporate evenly. While the blender is still on, slowly sprinkle in the xanthan gum to thicken and stabilize the mixture. Blend for another 30 seconds, then transfer to a resealable container.

Turn your ice cream maker on (I use the Kitchen-Aid ice cream maker attachment) and churn as per the machine's instructions. Once your ice cream has churned, return to the plastic container and place in the freezer for a few hours to set up.

To make the roasted figs, preheat the oven to 250°F.

Trim off the top of each fig, cut into halves, then place in a baking dish. Combine the melted butter and brown sugar, then pour on top of the figs. Boil 1 cup of water in a kettle, then add to the figs, stirring everything together. Place in the oven to roast very slowly for 2 to 2½ hours, or until softened and caramelized. You can deglaze the bottom of the baking dish with a few splashes of very hot water if you notice that some of the brown sugar and butter mixture is a bit stuck (this will also make an ad hoc sauce). These figs can be made the day before serving. Store them in the fridge and then bring them back to life with a splash of water over low heat in a pan. You can use fresh figs when they're available and in season, if you like; just roast them with a little less water.

To make the reduction, bring the grape vinegar and sugar to a boil in a small pot. Reduce for about 18 minutes, until the mixture cooks down to about ⅓ cup and is slightly thickened. To test, you can take a spoon

NOTE: Xanthan gum is essential for any homemade ice cream in my opinion. Not only does it thicken a no-cook mixture like this one, but it also stabilizes the mixture. It keeps the ice cream emulsified and prevents that gritty crystallization that can form in the freezer otherwise, keeping your ice cream smooth and luxurious. Also, feel free to use standard double cream instead of the ashta if you like.

and drop some of the reduction on a plate. Tilt the plate downward, and if it slowly trickles down and appears thickened (as opposed to running down the plate like a watery vinegar) you know you're there. Take the reduction off the heat and allow to cool. Transfer to a resealable plastic container or squeeze bottle and store in your fridge for up to 10 days.

To serve, scoop the ashta ice cream into bowls and top with some of the roasted figs and a drizzle of the grape vinegar reduction. If you are into sweet and savory desserts, you can sprinkle on some coarse sea salt as well!

ESSENTIALS

**CUCUMBER
AND GARLIC YOGURT**
(recipe on page 210)

DAKKA
(recipe on page 214)

TAHINI SAUCE
(recipe on page 210)

**GARLIC
MAYO**

HARISSA
(recipe on page 211)

SAFFRON BUTTER
(recipe on page 212)

BASIC LEMON VINAIGRETTE

MAKES 1¼ CUPS
PREP TIME: 10 MINUTES

A simple lemon vinaigrette dressing is exceptionally versatile, and remember—it's all about the right ratios of ingredients. I prefer my dressing on the tart side, but feel free to add another drop of olive oil to neutralize the flavor if you want. Make a batch of this vinaigrette each week, store it in a squeeze bottle or mason jar, then use it to dress salads or even drizzle on roasted chicken breasts and fish.

◆

⅔ cup + 3 Tbsp olive oil
⅓ cup lemon juice
1½ Tbsp honey
1 Tbsp Dijon mustard
¾ tsp salt

Combine all the ingredients in a large mixing bowl. It's helpful to measure the olive oil in your tablespoon before the honey. Whisk well to emulsify, then transfer to a squeeze bottle. Can be kept in the fridge for up to 1 week.

◆ ◆ ◆

GARLIC MAYO

MAKES 1¼ CUPS
PREP TIME: 10 MINUTES

Once you master a basic aioli, you'll find yourself adding different flavors (you can mix in herbs, spices, chilies, etc.) to suit the needs of so many savory dishes.

◆

2 cloves garlic, chopped
1 Tbsp Dijon mustard
1 Tbsp lemon juice
¾ tsp salt
2 egg yolks
¾ cup canola oil

Place the garlic, mustard, lemon juice, salt and egg yolks in a blender. Blend on low, then slowly drizzle in the oil in a thin line to emulsify. Be careful not to add to much at once, as this will break the emulsion. Loosen with 1 tablespoon of water to reach the desired consistency. This mayo can be kept for up to 1 week in a resealable plastic container or squeeze bottle.

CUCUMBER AND GARLIC YOGURT

MAKES 1¼ CUPS
PREP TIME: 10 MINUTES

When I was growing up, this condiment was a must with traditional stuffed grape leaves, and it's a perfect pairing for so many rich recipes in this book. Dollop some beside Teta Aida's Kofta (page 139), Lamb Shoulder Fattah with Orzo and Crisped Pita (page 159), or even spread onto the Yogurt-Braised Shortrib Shawarma (page 83) for a cooling tang that offsets the hearty flavors of the meat.

◆

2 baby cucumbers, finely chopped
1 cup plain Greek yogurt
1 clove garlic, minced
½ tsp salt
½ bunch mint, finely chopped

Combine all of the ingredients in a mixing bowl and store for up to 3 days in a resealable plastic container.

◆ ◆ ◆

TAHINI SAUCE

MAKES 2½ CUPS
PREP TIME: 5 MINUTES

Look, I'll be honest with this one—you can drizzle this sauce on pretty much any savory recipe in this entire book. It's that versatile and should be a staple for your fridge.

◆

1 cup tahini
½ cup lemon juice
½ tsp salt

Whisk all of the ingredients together in a bowl, along with up to 1 cup of water to emulsify (depending on how thick your tahini is). Transfer to a squeeze bottle or resealable plastic container and refrigerate up to 1 week.

HARISSA

A batch of homemade harissa belongs in your fridge, ready to add spicy tomato flavor anytime. Aside from all the uses in this book, mix it with ketchup for a grilled cheese sandwich, add it to sauces, create vibrant marinades, and even serve it straight up as a condiment for diners to add to their plates for extra kick.

◆

2–3 dried red chilies
1 red pepper
2 Tbsp olive oil
1 onion, minced
3 cloves garlic, minced
1 Tbsp cumin seeds
1 Tbsp coriander seeds
1 Tbsp caraway seeds
One 6 oz can tomato paste
1 tsp salt
1 Tbsp lemon juice

Rehydrate the red chilies (adding more if you like extra heat) in a bowl of hot water.

Roast the red pepper over an open flame, or place in a 450°F oven until blackened, about 15 minutes, turning regularly. Transfer to a bowl and cover tightly with plastic wrap. Allow the pepper to steam for several minutes, then remove the skin.

Heat the olive oil in a large skillet over medium heat. Sweat the onion and garlic for 6 to 7 minutes. Add the cumin, coriander, and caraway seeds and continue to cook for 1 minute. Add the tomato paste and cook until the onion is totally softened and the paste is no longer raw, another 1 to 2 minutes.

In a blender, combine the onion mixture with the roasted red pepper, chilies, and salt. Blend until smooth and finish with the lemon juice.

Transfer to a resealable plastic container or squeeze bottle. This will keep in the fridge for 1 week.

SAFFRON BUTTER

MAKES 1 CUP
PREP TIME: 5 MINUTES
COOK TIME: 10 MINUTES

It's a well-known fact that saffron is the most expensive spice in the world, with each thread being collected by hand, so there's no use in wasting a single gram. This butter is handy for finishing pastas, basting a roasted piece of fish, or even folding into a puree, always adding a pop of color and a sweet yet slightly bitter flavor. Keep this compound butter in your fridge door and reach for it any time a dish needs some uplifting—it's worth the cost.

◆

1 cup butter
1 tsp saffron threads

Melt the butter and saffron in a saucepan over medium-low heat. Turn off the heat and allow the mixture to infuse for 5 to 10 minutes.

Transfer to a blender and blend until very smooth. Transfer to a resealable plastic container and allow to cool, then refrigerate for up to 10 days.

◆ ◆ ◆

EGYPTIAN RICE

SERVES 4–6
PREP TIME: 20 MINUTES
COOK TIME: 22 MINUTES

This side dish is such a staple that it has a place on the table alongside the vast majority of the savory dishes in the book. It might seem a bit strange to combine pieces of toasted vermicelli with the rice, but once you try it, I think you'll love the contrast in color and flavor that it provides.

◆

1 cup white medium-grain rice
1 Tbsp butter
1 Tbsp olive oil
1 cup vermicelli, broken into
　small pieces
1 tsp salt

First wash all of the starch off the rice. Place the rice in a strainer and run under cold water, then transfer to a bowl of cold water. Allow the rice to sit for a few minutes before repeating the process again. Repeat 3 to 4 times until the water is clear and no longer foggy from the starch—this will take about 20 to 25 minutes in total. Drain the rinsed rice.

In a large pot, heat the butter and olive oil over medium-low heat. Add the vermicelli and toast for 3 to 5 minutes until deeply golden. Add the rice and toast for another minute. Add 2½ cups water and the salt and bring to a boil. Reduce to a simmer, cover, and cook for 15 to 17 minutes until cooked through. Take off the heat and let sit, covered, for 5 minutes. Fluff with a fork, then serve.

◆ ◆ ◆

LEBANESE TOUM

MAKES 2½ CUPS
PREP TIME: 10 MINUTES

You know when you go to your local shawarma place and the person behind the counter asks if you want "garlic"? They're referring to the white, garlicky spread that inevitably ends up being slathered across the bottom of your pita before the other fillings join in. Well, the "garlic" in question is this pungent spread, and it is a must for your repertoire. Often this emulsion is made without the aid of an egg white, but quite frankly, it's a bit tricky to do unless you're making a huge batch.

◆

20 cloves garlic
1 tsp salt
1 egg white
2 Tbsp lemon juice, divided
1⅓ cups canola oil
⅓ cup ice water

Place the garlic, salt, egg white, and 1 tablespoon of the lemon juice in the bowl of a food processor. Blitz until foamy and totally incorporated. With the blender running, drizzle in half the oil slowly to emulsify. Add the remaining lemon juice. Continue to add the remaining oil until the mixture is thick and stable. Thin out with ice water to your desired consistency.

Store in an airtight container in the fridge for up to 10 days.

DAKKA

MAKES 2½ CUPS
PREP TIME: 15 MINUTES
COOK TIME: 25 MINUTES

1 Tbsp olive oil
6 cloves garlic, minced
3 bird's-eye chilies, minced
¼ tsp ground coriander
¼ tsp ground cumin
2 Tbsp white vinegar
½ tsp salt
1 cup beef or vegetable stock
½ cup cilantro, finely chopped
1½ Tbsp lemon juice

I came up with this play on one of the must-have condiments of Middle Eastern cooking for Koshary with Red Lentil Ragù (page 156). Use this spicy and tangy sauce to embolden any fatty and savory dish that could use some excitement.

◆

Heat the olive oil in a large pot over low heat and sweat the garlic and chilies for 2 to 3 minutes. Add the coriander and cumin and toast for another minute. Then add the vinegar, salt, stock, and 1 cup water, and bring to a boil. Lower the heat and simmer for about 20 minutes.

Take off the heat and stir in the cilantro. Allow the dakka to cool, then add the lemon juice to keep its flavor bright.

Store in a resealable container for up to 5 days.

RAS EL HANOUT

MAKES ½ CUP
PREP TIME: 15 MINUTES

Making your own complex spice blend is worth the time required to toast, grind, and combine all of the different elements. You can find ready-made ras el hanout these days, but it's always better to control the freshness and exact flavor profile to your taste (not to mention it's much cheaper to make it yourself). I love this North African spice blend on everything from roasted fish and poultry to vegetables, or mixed into yogurt for a quick condiment.

◆

2 Tbsp coriander seeds
2 tsp cumin seeds
2 tsp fennel seeds
1 tsp fenugreek
½ tsp chili flakes
10 cardamom pods
2 tsp cinnamon
2 tsp sweet paprika
1 tsp Aleppo pepper
1 tsp dried mint
½ tsp ginger
½ tsp turmeric
½ tsp white pepper
¼ tsp clove
¼ tsp mace

In a large skillet, toast the coriander, cumin, fennel, fenugreek, chili flakes, and cardamom pods over medium-low heat until fragrant, 2 to 3 minutes.

Grind the spices but don't overdo it. I like to keep a little bit of texture.

In a bowl, combine the ground spices with the remaining spices, whisking to combine evenly.

Store in a resealable plastic container for up to 1 month.

LABNEH WITH GARLIC CONFIT

MAKES 1½ CUPS

PREP TIME: 5 MINUTES, PLUS OVERNIGHT FOR DRAINING

COOK TIME: 2 HOURS

3 cups plain yogurt
1½ tsp salt
15 cloves garlic
1 cup olive oil

Magic happens when you simply salt some yogurt and wait. This makes a tangy, incredibly delicious dip or side to any of the meats in this book. The addition of the garlic in the labneh, along with some on top, makes for a more interesting flavor and presentation.

◆

In a large mixing bowl, combine the yogurt and the salt. Line a fine-mesh strainer with some cheesecloth, then place on top of another bowl. Transfer the salted yogurt to the lined strainer, and refrigerate overnight.

Preheat the oven to 250°F. Place the garlic in an ovenproof skillet. Cover with the olive oil and bake for 2 hours. Remove the garlic with a slotted spoon and set aside. Also, save the amazing garlic-infused oil!

The next day, when the labneh has thickened, transfer to a separate bowl and mix with 5 or 6 cloves of the roasted garlic. Top with a few additional cloves when ready to serve, and drizzle on some of the garlic oil for extra richness.

DUKKAH

MAKES 1⅓ CUPS
PREP TIME: 15 MINUTES
COOK TIME: 5 MINUTES

This is what happens when spices, nuts, and dried herbs all come together to make a vibrant condiment. Egyptian dukkah is commonly used as a dip or versatile spice blend. Feel free to combine your blend with olive oil for dipping pitas, or sprinkle on your favorite roasted vegetable, fish, or even cheese with a drizzle of honey. My version substitutes macadamia nuts for the traditional hazelnuts, but feel free to experiment with different combinations of your own!

◆

1 Tbsp cumin seeds
1 Tbsp coriander seeds
1 Tbsp caraway seeds
1 Tbsp fennel seeds
½ cup almonds
½ cup macadamia nuts
1 Tbsp dried mint
1 tsp kalonji or nigella seeds
1 tsp smoked paprika
1 tsp smoked salt
½ tsp sumac
¼ cup sesame seeds

Start by toasting your cumin, coriander, caraway, and fennel seeds in a dry skillet over medium-low heat. Use all of your senses when toasting whole spices: smell the aromas come alive, watch the seeds start to brown, and even listen to them start to pop. This can take 4 to 5 minutes, with occasional stirring and tossing.

In a separate pan, toast the nuts and look for all of the same qualities. The nuts will brown and become aromatic.

Add the ingredients to the food processor, paying attention to the order. We want the appropriate texture for all of the ingredients, and we definitely don't want to create a nut butter. Add the toasted seeds to the food processor and pulse until very fine. Then add the mint, kalonji seeds, paprika, smoked salt, and sumac. Process further until everything is well combined and fine. Add the nuts next. Pulse carefully in increments. Watch to make sure that the texture of the nuts becomes fine, but not a pureed nut butter. This will only take a few pulses, and make sure to scrape along the sides between each pulse. Add the sesame seeds and pulse a few more times.

Transfer to a resealable plastic container and keep refrigerated for up to 1 month.

ROSEWATER WHIPPED CREAM

MAKES 2 CUPS

PREP TIME: 5 MINUTES, PLUS 2 HOURS FOR SETTING

The tricks for perfect handmade whipped cream are quite simple: under-whip the cream a bit so it stays velvety (it will firm up more in the fridge), use high-quality vanilla, and add just the right amount of sugar so that it's not too sweet.

◆

1 cup whipping cream

¼ cup sugar

1 Tbsp vanilla bean paste, or 1 tsp vanilla extract

Pinch salt

¼ tsp rosewater

Place your cream in a large bowl and begin to whisk in some air. Once you've formed soft peaks, add the sugar, vanilla, and salt. Whisk until you achieve a medium peak (not quite firm enough to hold the bowl upside down over your head). Stir in the rosewater and transfer to a resealable container.

Store in the fridge for at least 2 hours to allow the cream to firm up ever so slightly.

PISTACHIO BUTTER

MAKES ABOUT 1¾ CUPS
PREP TIME: 5 MINUTES
COOK TIME: 10 MINUTES

Never have just two ingredients created something so special. This pistachio butter works in the dessert world, but it also comes in handy for many savory dishes as well. It's great paired with roasted beets, on toasted bread with cheese, and as part of the filling for a delectable tart.

◆

1¼ cups shelled pistachios
⅓ cup sweetened condensed milk

Preheat the oven to 350°F. Place the pistachios in a single layer on a baking sheet and toast in the oven for 7 to 8 minutes, until aromatic.

Place the pistachios in a food processor. Blitz until the pistachios are very fine and almost turning into a butter. Add the sweetened condensed milk and continue to pulse. The mixture will become very thick and very smooth. Add ⅓ cup water to loosen the mixture and process until well combined.

Transfer to a resealable plastic container and store in the fridge but return to room temperature before serving. Good for up to 10 days.

FETEER DOUGH

MAKES 4–6 PORTIONS

PREP TIME: 20 MINUTES, PLUS
1 HOUR TO OVERNIGHT FOR
RESTING

This is a very basic dough, but the magic happens when you develop gluten then allow it to rest. The final dough can be gently stretched and encouraged into a nearly translucent thinness on your work surface. This provides a fun opportunity to paint the thin dough with clarified butter, then stuff with either savory or sweet fillings.

◆

4 cups all-purpose flour

2 cups warm water

¾ tsp salt

½ cup olive oil, divided

Combine the flour, water, and salt in a stand mixer using the dough hook attachment. Knead the dough on a medium speed for 12 to 15 minutes. The dough should form a ball and clean the sides of the mixing bowl, meaning that the gluten has been activated and the dough is strong.

Grease a baking sheet with ¼ cup of the olive oil. Divide the dough into 4 or 6 balls (depending on which recipe you are using it for) and place on the oiled sheet. Top the dough balls with the remaining ¼ cup of olive oil. Cover and allow to rest at least 1 hour, but preferably overnight in the fridge.

CHUNKY EGYPTIAN TOMATO SAUCE

MAKES 3 CUPS
PREP TIME: 10 MINUTES
COOK TIME: 35 MINUTES

This recipe adds some character to a basic tomato sauce with the addition of spices and red pepper. I always make sure to have canned tomatoes (in a pinch, use passata) on hand in my pantry, as the sauce is perfect when paired with roasted vegetables or shakshuka and served over rice or tossed with pasta.

◆

¼ cup olive oil
4 cloves garlic, minced
½ red onion, diced
1 red pepper, diced
2 tsp smoked paprika
1 tsp ground cumin
1 tsp ground coriander
½ tsp Aleppo pepper
¼ tsp chili flakes
¼ cup tomato paste
One 26 oz can chopped tomatoes
½ tsp salt

Heat the olive oil in a large saucepan over low heat, then sweat the garlic, onion, and red pepper for 7 to 8 minutes, until slightly softened. Add the smoked paprika, cumin, coriander, Aleppo pepper, and chili flakes and cook for 1 to 2 minutes. Then add the tomato paste and cook for an additional minute. Add the chopped tomatoes, 1 cup water, and salt, and bring to a boil. Reduce to a simmer and cook for about 20 minutes, until reduced slightly. Can be kept for up to 3 days in the fridge and reheated upon serving.

EGYPTIAN WHOLE WHEAT BALADI BREAD

MAKES 6 LOAVES

PREP TIME: 25 MINUTES, PLUS
2 HOURS FOR PROOFING

COOK TIME: 30 MINUTES

You're only a handful of ingredients away from creating a home version of the Egyptian staple bread—baladi. This bread is so important to Egyptian culture that the country's government once famously subsidized the cost to its citizens, making sure that everyone could afford their daily supply. By blasting the temperature and cooking in the hottest place in your oven (the floor!) you'll quickly add this nutty, puffy whole wheat pita to your regular baking repertoire.

◆

2 tsp active dry yeast

1 tsp sugar

3 cups whole wheat flour

1 tsp salt

⅓ cup wheat bran, for coating
(see note)

Heat 1¾ cups water until it's warm to the touch but not uncomfortable to hold your finger in (usually between 105°F and 110°F if you're using a thermometer). Add the yeast and sugar, and let bloom for about 10 minutes, or until the mixture is foamy.

Mix the whole wheat flour and salt in a stand mixer bowl to incorporate. Add the water and yeast mixture, stirring just until the mixture comes together. Attach the dough hook, then knead on medium-low speed for 16 to 18 minutes. The mixture will appear wet at first, but don't worry; it will come together. Fight the temptation to add more flour, because you want the dough to be moist so it can puff up.

Transfer the dough to a greased bowl and cover with a kitchen towel. Allow to rise in a warm place in your kitchen for 1½ hours. The dough will increase in volume, but not necessarily double in size.

Transfer the dough to your work surface and divide into 6 even pieces. Bring the corners of each piece together, then roll into a small ball. Repeat until all of the pieces have been formed into balls, then place on a baking sheet and cover loosely with a kitchen towel. Proof for 30 minutes.

Remove the bottom rack in the oven and preheat to 500°F. Line a baking sheet with parchment paper.

Flip over each ball and coat what was the bottom side with a sprinkling of wheat bran. Working in batches and keeping the unused balls covered with the kitchen towel to keep them from drying out, flatten the balls into ¼-inch-thick rounds 5 to 6 inches in diameter. Place 2 pitas at a time on the lined baking sheet and place on the floor of the oven, or

on the lowest rack possible. Bake for 5 to 6 minutes until the pitas have puffed up, then transfer to the top rack for an additional 2 to 3 minutes to finish cooking. Repeat until all of the pitas have been baked.

To replicate the char of a hot oven, you can take the cooked pitas and heat a cast-iron or nonstick skillet over high heat. Place the cooked pitas, wheat bran side down, in the skillet and toast for 45 seconds to 1 minute. Enjoy immediately or reheat in a low oven at time of serving.

◆

NOTE: Look for wheat bran in a bulk food store or the specialty aisle in your grocery store. It's the outer layer of the wheat kernel, and it gives baladi bread its distinctive nutty flavor and texture. The recipe still works well if you can't find it, but it's worth looking for.

EGYPTIAN CHICKEN STOCK

MAKES 2 QUARTS
PREP TIME: 10 MINUTES
COOK TIME: 2–3 HOURS

3 Tbsp canola oil

2 lb chicken bones

2 white onions, roughly chopped
  with skins on

3 heads garlic, halved widthwise

2 stalks celery, roughly chopped

1 Tbsp tomato paste

1 Tbsp coriander seeds

1 Tbsp cumin seeds

12 cardamom pods

1 tsp whole allspice

2 pieces mastic (optional, see note)

½ bunch thyme

2 bay leaves

I always keep a batch of chicken stock on hand, even freezing some into ice cubes. Egyptian chicken stock is defined by its traditional spices and the addition of a touch of mastic.

◆

Heat the canola oil in a large stockpot over high heat and add the chicken bones. Sear until deeply browned, 8 to 10 minutes, then remove. Add the onions, garlic, and celery and reduce the heat to medium, stirring for 1 to 2 minutes. Add the tomato paste and cook for another minute. Add the coriander, cumin, cardamom, allspice, mastic, thyme, and bay leaves. Add the bones back to the pot and cover with 10 cups water.

Bring to a boil, then reduce the heat until the mixture barely simmers. Gently cook for 2 to 3 hours until the stock has slightly reduced and darkened, then strain.

Allow the strained stock to cool completely before storing in resealable plastic containers that are suitable for freezing or the fridge. Stock is good for up to 4 days in the fridge, or 6 months in the freezer.

◆

NOTE: Mastic is also known as *mesteka* and can be found in Middle Eastern grocery stores (though you'll probably have to ask for it). The recipe calls for just 2 little pieces, and trust me, that's all you need! The cedar, pine, and minty impact of each little morsel is dramatic. Also, never season your stock with salt. A good chicken stock is the building block of other dishes, which should be seasoned later on.

NOT TOO SWEET, NOT TOO SPICY HALVA

MAKES 2 CUPS
PREP TIME: 5 MINUTES, PLUS TIME FOR RESTING THE DOUGH
COOK TIME: 5 MINUTES

1 cup tahini
1 tsp baking powder
1 tsp ground coriander
½ tsp ground cumin
½ tsp salt
¼ tsp cinnamon
¼ tsp chili flakes
½ cup sugar

Initially I set out to work on a halva recipe to include as a dessert, or as an exclusively sweet topping for something like yogurt. But then something came over me and I thought, why not cut the sweetness and include a little spice for an interesting twist? This halva has half the sugar of a traditional version, and the right number of savory elements, making it a unique snack and flaky topping for roasted vegetables.

◆

In a large mixing bowl, combine the tahini, baking powder, coriander, cumin, salt, cinnamon, and chili flakes. Whisk well to combine, and make sure to use a bowl that has enough room for the mixture to expand when the hot sugar is added.

Line a baking sheet with parchment paper.

In a saucepan, combine the sugar and ½ cup water over medium-high heat. Bring the sugar to the hardball stage. If you have a candy thermometer, you're looking for 260°F. If you don't have a candy thermometer, the hardball stage is just before the clear sugar takes on a slight caramel hue. It will also thicken because the hardball stage means that most of the water has boiled away. This is a key step because without it, the halva won't stiffen and develop that distinctive crumbly texture.

When the sugar has reached the hardball stage, immediately transfer it to the bowl with the tahini mixture, whisking vigorously.

Pour the mixture onto the lined baking sheet, and allow to firm up in the fridge for at least 2 hours. The halva can then be broken into smaller pieces and stored in a resealable plastic container in the fridge for up to 1 month.

ACKNOWLEDGMENTS

WRITING A COOKBOOK HAS PROVEN to be an all-encompassing project—one that has captured my entire attention, focus, and time. For the better part of the past two years, I've been consistently cooking, writing, testing, and stressing; sometimes all at the same time. It is for this reason that I have to thank my wife, Mila, for not divorcing me, killing me, or both in that order. She has been a rock of understanding and patience, and has even proved to be a qualified taste tester. Throughout it all, she not only put up with this exhausting process, but she also knew when to remind me that it would all work out in the end. Thank you, Neenie (oh shut up, as if you don't have a cute pet name for your spouse!), I love you.

A huge thank you once again to my parents, who have always supported my culinary journey. It was tough at first, but they never wavered in their love and support, and for that I feel so lucky and grateful. A special thanks to my mom specifically for working with me on a lot of these recipes. Whenever I had a question or needed a reminder about an old family tradition, she was there to share her years of experience.

Thanks to my brother and all my friends who cheered me on, visiting every restaurant and watching every show that I was a part of. Your encouragement throughout the years really kept me going, especially during those early days when I needed it most. A special thank you to the entire Gill family for always supporting me, the Morris family, and of course to my dear friend Dr. Tarek Shaarawy for all of his insight into true Egyptian and Middle Eastern cuisine.

A very special thank you to Chef Cruz Goler and the team at Lupa. I was so lucky to have stumbled into your kitchen to begin my career. You all showed me what it took to be a professional in this industry, and your lessons were the fabric of each good habit that I established early on. Thanks to all of the great chefs, cooks, and restaurateurs that continued to teach me as

well: the Jean-Georges Vongerichten opening team at the Mark Hotel, the entire team at the International Culinary Center (including my inspiring classmates—Lindsay King, Rhoda Boone Lane, Christine Flynn, Adam Bordonaro, Ashley Coyte, Jonas Ladao, Nardelys Gonzalez, Mike Wong, Lindsay Hunt, Cara Faye Earl, Mick Markley, Scott Shulman, Jessica Kanat, Dean Sheremet, and Bam Suppipat), Chef Doug Neigel, Chef Steve Gouzopoulos, David Minicucci, and Steve Kalogiros.

Thank you to Portia Corman for making my wildest dream come true. Not a lot of people get to live out their childhood dreams, and I was only able to because she believed in me enough to cast me as a national television host. As if that weren't enough, she has become an honest, caring, and trustworthy friend who is always looking out for me. I wouldn't be here if not for you, Portia. Thanks also to the whole team at the CBC, especially to my friend and TV mentor Steven Sabados. Thank you to Marilyn Denis and her team as well for allowing me to continue to share my passion for cooking with Canadians from coast to coast.

Thank you to Tony Tavares and his entire team at Butterball Canada. Tony hired me to be his spokesperson *before* I was discovered for a TV gig! He always had such belief in me and has supported me in ways that I could never repay. He has become someone that I look up to as a personal and business mentor, and I can't thank him enough. Thank you as well to René Proulx and the Exceldor team for always making me feel like an important part of the group.

It's not often that you befriend a former high school teacher, but that's exactly what happened with Bob Goldman. Mr. Goldman not only wrote the reference letter that got me into the Schulich School of Business (he's that good a writer, because I assure you my grades weren't that great) but he also coached me through the writing portion of this process. Thanks, Bob, for all of the proofreading and feedback.

The amazing editors and team at Appetite by Random House deserve a ton of thanks as well. To Robert McCullough, Lindsay Paterson, and Zoe Maslow—thank you for this incredible opportunity and for all of your support throughout. Thanks to Emma Dolan for her incredible work in designing such a beautiful book. Thank you also to the dynamic duo at Benson & Oak: Kyla Zanardi and Houston Mausner, along with the prop styling talents of Rayna Marlee Schwartz, for creating truly amazing photography.

Last but not least, thanks to you—the reader. I am so fortunate to have the chance to share my passion with people, and it's a privilege that I don't take for granted. So I genuinely want to thank you for choosing my book—I hope it inspired you to experiment with Middle Eastern flavors and maybe even encouraged you to follow your dreams.

With sincere gratitude,

Shahir

INDEX

Aleppo pepper
  about, 9
  and honey butter with
    sweet potatoes, 113
almonds
  Dukkah, 218
  Summer Green Bean Fasolia, 106
  Sweet and Spiced Nut Medley,
    58
anise/aniseed
  about, 9
  Kahk Cookies, 197
  Manakeesh with Lamb and
    Yogurt, 87
  Za'atar Spread, 87
apples, maple-glazed, 189–90
apricot
  and honey syrup, 194
  mishmish, 194
apricot jam: Aunt Susie's Famous
  Star Cookies, 179
Arctic char, hibiscus-cured with
  labneh, 30
artichokes, grilled, with tomato
  béchamel and garlic crisps,
  124–25
arugula
  and lemon emulsion, 62
  Seared Halloumi and Orange-
    Glazed Beet Salad, 118
ashta ice cream, 204–5

baba ghanoush, tarragon, 70
baking, about, 12–13
baladi
  Egyptian whole wheat bread,
    224–25
  three pepper, 110
basbousa, brown butter and
  coconut, 193
basturma, "shortcut," 101
beans. See fava beans; green bean
  fasolia; white beans
beef
  cheek, braised, bil basal, 151
  hawawshi sandwiches, 88

rib eye, reverse-seared, 160
ribs, with pomegranate
  barbecue sauce, 144
sambousek, 94–96
shortrib shawarma, yogurt-
  braised, 83
steak tartare, Middle Eastern,
  with lemon sabayon, 69
beets
  dip, pink and gold, 50
  orange-glazed, and halloumi
    salad, 118
  Vinegar-Glazed Turnips with
    Dukkah, 128
bil basal, braised beef cheek, 151
bison and lamb kofta, 139
black lime powder, and rack of
  lamb with cured olive pan
  sauce, 172
blue cheese: Mom's Cheese
  Squares, 46
boftek, veal chop, with kohlrabi
  and pomegranate salad, 148
bread. See also buns; sandwiches
  calf liver on toast, 92
  Egyptian whole wheat baladi,
    224–25
  fino, with tahini and molasses,
    38–39
  ful breakfast, 22
  Hibiscus-Cured Arctic Char
    with Labneh, 30
  Manakeesh with Lamb and
    Yogurt, 87
  Seared Halloumi and Orange-
    Glazed Beet Salad, 118
  Sourdough Om Ali Bread
    Pudding with Coconut
    Sauce, 183
  Walnut Sauce, 162–63
breadcrumbs: Spiced Rice, 66–67
bulgur: Dehydrated Tomato and
  Parsley Tabbouleh Salad, 131
buns
  Fried Shrimp Sandwiches, 80
  Seared Falafel Burgers, 76–77

burgers, seared falafel, 76–77
buttermilk
  Glazed Orange and Spice Olive
    Oil Cake, 25
  Parsley Sauce, 105
  Stuffed Arabic Pancakes with
    Maple-Glazed Apples,
    189–90
butters
  brown, 75
  honey, and Aleppo pepper
    with sweet potatoes, 113
  parsley hot, 155
  pistachio, 221
  saffron, 212

cakes
  Brown Butter and Coconut
    Basbousa, 193
  glazed orange and spice olive
    oil, 25
calamari, grilled, with tomato jam,
  171
cannelloni: Macarona Béchamel
  with Veal Ragù, 167–68
caraway seeds
  about, 9
  Dukkah, 218
  Harissa, 211
  Seared Falafel Burgers, 76–77
  Spiced Rice, 66–67
cardamom
  about, 10
  Egyptian Chicken Stock,
    226
  Lamb Shoulder Fattah with
    Orzo and Crisped Pita, 159
  Ras El Hanout, 215
  Spinach and Kale Mulukhiyah
    with Crisped and Spiced
    Rabbit, 75
  Whipped Feta with Eggplant
    Relish, 56–57
carob molasses cookies, 184
carrots, triple-sesame with goat
  cheese, 134

cashews: Mixed Mushroom and Rice Loaf with Chanterelle Cream, 165–66
cauliflower and turmeric bites, 45
chard, rainbow, braised, with taro chips, 127
chard, Swiss: Green Sauce, 132–33
cherry and wine compote, 180–81
chicken. *See also* Cornish hen
  sharkaseya with walnut sauce and crackling, 162–63
  stock, Egyptian, 226
  thighs, harissa with saffron Israeli couscous, 175
  wings, baked, with sumac and parsley hot butter, 155
chicken livers, mousse, 60–61
chickpea flour: Chickpea Fries with Harissa Mayo, 53
chickpeas
  crispy, 156
  and tomato halabissa soup, 91
cilantro
  Beef Hawawshi Sandwiches, 88
  Blistered Okra with Green Sauce and Baked Cheese, 132–33
  Braised Rainbow Chard with Taro Chips, 127
  Dakka, 214
  Gido Habib's Ful Breakfast, 22
  Green Sauce, 132–33
  Grilled Calamari with Tomato Jam, 171
  Grilled Whole Fish with Yellow Pepper Vinaigrette and Charred Scallions, 143
  Middle Eastern Steak Tartare with Lemon Sabayon, 69
  Reverse-Seared Rib Eye with Dakka, 160
  Seared Falafel Burgers, 76–77
  Three Pepper Baladi Salad, 110
coconut
  and brown butter basbousa, 193
  glaze, 193
coconut milk: Coconut Sauce, 183
cod, roasted sayadieh, with couscous and pan sauce, 152

coffee and coriander rub, 144
compote, strawberry and orange blossom, 48–49
cookies
  Aunt Susie's Famous Star Cookies, 179
  carob molasses, 184
  digestive, crust, 187–88
  kahk, 197
coriander seeds
  about, 10
  Arabic Coffee and Coriander Beef Ribs with Pomegranate Barbecue Sauce, 144
  Braised Rainbow Chard with Taro Chips, 127
  Chickpea Fries with Harissa Mayo, 53
  Dukkah, 218
  Eggplant Relish, 56–57
  Egyptian Chicken Stock, 226
  Harissa, 211
  Ras El Hanout, 215
  Reverse-Seared Rib Eye with Dakka, 160
  Seared Falafel Burgers, 76–77
  Spiced Rice, 66–67
  Spinach and Kale Mulukhiyah with Crisped and Spiced Rabbit, 75
  Whipped Feta with Eggplant Relish, 56–57
corned beef: Five-Hour "Shortcut" Basturma, 101
Cornish hen, with lemon and black cumin, 146–47
cornmeal: Turmeric Fayesh, 34
couscous
  and roasted cod sayadieh, 152
  saffron Israeli, 175
cream, chanterelle, 165–66
cream cheese
  Apricot Mishmish, 194
  cheese squares, 46
  Classic Konafa with Wine and Cherry Compote, 180–81
cucumber
  Dehydrated Tomato and Parsley Tabbouleh Salad, 131

and garlic yogurt, 210
Heirloom Tomato Fattoush Salad, 105
Three Pepper Baladi Salad, 110
cumin. *See also* cumin, black
  about, 10
  Crispy Cauliflower and Turmeric Bits, 45
  Dukkah, 218
  eggs, 65
  Egyptian Chicken Stock, 226
  Gido Habib's Ful Breakfast, 22
  Harissa, 211
  Seared Falafel Burgers, 76–77
  Spiced Rice, 66–67
  Whipped Feta with Eggplant Relish, 56–57
cumin, black, and grilled Cornish hen with lemon, 146–47

dairy, about, 12
dakka, 214
dates
  Kahk Cookies, 197
  Sourdough Om Ali Bread Pudding with Coconut Sauce, 183
date vinegar glaze, 60–61
dill
  Hibiscus-Cured Arctic Char with Labneh, 30
  Seared Falafel Burgers, 76–77
  Spiced Rice and Yellow Zucchini Mahshi, 109
  Vinegar-Glazed Turnips with Dukka, 128
dill pickles: Yogurt-Braised Shortrib Shawarma, 83
dips and spreads
  Black and White Hummus with Sun-Dried Tomato and Caramelized Lemon, 42–43
  Chicken Liver Mousse with Date Vinegar Glaze, 60–61
  Mahlab Foie Gras with Strawberry and Orange Blossom Compote, 48–49
  Pink and Gold Beet Dip with Pine Nuts, 50

Tarragon Baba Ghanoush, 70
  Za'atar Spread, 87
dough
  for Beef Sambousek, 94–96
  feteer, 222
duck, mulberry-glazed with ginger
    and cherry freekah, 140–41
dukkah
homemade, 218
  sweet and savory brittle, 201
  and vinegar-glazed turnips, 128

edamame: Seared Falafel Burgers,
    76–77
eggah, stuffed, with feta, 36–37
eggplant
  baba ghanoush, tarragon, 70
  relish, and whipped feta, 56–57
  tomato-glazed, with broiled
    cream, 121
eggs
  about, 12
  Crispy Grape Leaves with
    Braised Lamb and Spiced
    Rice, 66–67
  cumin, 65
  Egyptian Rice Pudding with
    Fall Spices and Orange, 29
  ful breakfast, 22
  Lemon Sabayon, 69
  Mixed Mushroom and Rice
    Loaf with Chanterelle
    Cream, 165–66
  Pistachio Tart with Cookie
    Crust, Wild Blueberries, and
    Olive Oil, 187–88
  shakshuka, 26
  Sourdough Om Ali Bread
    Pudding with Coconut
    Sauce, 183
  stuffed eggah with feta, 36–37

falafel burgers, 76–77
fattah, lamb shoulder with orzo
    and pita, 159
fava beans
  about, 22
  ful breakfast, 22
fayesh, turmeric, 34

fennel, ground: Spicy Turkey
    Feteer, 97–98
fennel seeds
  Crispy Grape Leaves with
    Braised Lamb and Spiced
    Rice, 66–67
  Dukkah, 218
  Spiced Rice, 66–67
fenugreek
  about, 10
  Five-Hour "Shortcut"
    Basturma, 101
feta cheese
  and stuffed eggah, 36–37
  Three Pepper Baladi Salad, 110
  whipped, with eggplant relish,
    56–57
feteer
  dough, 222
  spicy turkey, 97–98
  with wildflower honey and
    cinnamon, 202
figs, roasted, 204–5
fino bread, with tahini and
    molasses, 38–39
fish. See also Arctic char; cod;
    grouper
  grilled whole, with yellow
    pepper vinaigrette and
    charred scallions, 143
flatbread: ful breakfast, 22
foie gras, mahlab, with strawberry
    and orange blossom compote,
    48–49
freekah, cherry, and mulberry-
    glazed duck with ginger,
    140–41
fries, chickpea, 53
fruits, dried, about, 13

garlic
  and cucumber yogurt, 210
  Dakka, 214
  Egyptian Chicken Stock, 226
  Lebanese Toum, 213
garlic crisps, 124–25
garlic mayonnaise, 209
glazes
  coconut, 193

date vinegar, 60–61
  mango, 54
grape leaves, with braised lamb and
    spiced rice, 66–67
grape vinegar reduction, 204–5
green bean fasolia, 106
green pepper relish, 92
grouper, crudo, with arugula and
    lemon emulsion, 62

halloumi, seared, and orange-
    glazed beet salad, 118
halva, sweet and spicy, 229
harissa
  Beef Hawawshi Sandwiches,
    88
  chicken thighs with saffron
    Israeli couscous, 175
  homemade, 211
  mayo, 53
  Middle Eastern Steak with
    Lemon Sabayon, 69
herbs, about, 11–12
hibiscus-cured Arctic char with
    labneh, 30
honey
  and apricot syrup, 194
  butter, 113
hummus, black and white, with
    sun-dried tomato and
    caramelized lemon, 42–43

iceberg lettuce
  Fried Shrimp Sandwiches, 80
  Yogurt-Braised Shortrib
    Shawarma, 83
ice cream, ashta, with roasted figs
    and grape vinegar reduction,
    204–5
icing sugar. See powdered sugar
ingredients
  notes about, 14
  for pantry, 9–12

jam
  quince, 33
  tomato, 171

kahk cookies, 197

kale
    and leek khisk, 79
    and spinach mulukhiyah with
      rabbit, 75
kefir: Yogurt-Braised Shortrib
    Shawarma, 83
kitchen equipment, 16–17
kofta, Teta Aida's, 139
kohlrabi and pomegranate salad,
    148
konafa, classic, with wine and
    cherry compote, 180–81
koshary, with red lentil ragù, 156

labneh
    with garlic confit, 217
    and hibiscus-cured Arctic char, 30
    and potato salad with lentils, 122
lamb
    and bison kofta, 139
    braised, with spiced rice and
      grape leaves, 66–67
    manakeesh with yogurt, 87
    rack, black lime with cured
      olive pan sauce, 172
    shoulder fattah, with orzo and
      pita, 159
leek soup, with kale and onions, 79
lemons
    and arugula emulsion, 62
    basic vinaigrette, 209
    caramelized, and hummus and
      sun-dried tomato, 42–43
    sabayon, 69
lentils, beluga, and fingerling
    potato salad, 122
lentils, red
    ragù, 156
    soup, 84
liver, calf, on toast, 92

macadamia nuts: Dukkah, 218
macarona béchamel, with veal
    ragù, 167–68
mahlab
    about, 10
    Kahk Cookies, 197
mahshi, spiced rice and yellow
    zucchini, 109

manakeesh with lamb and yogurt,
    87
mango juice: Mango-Glazed Olives
    and Sun-Dried Tomatoes, 54
mascarpone: Stuffed Arabic
    Pancakes with Maple-Glazed
    Apples, 189–90
mayonnaise
    garlic, 209
    harissa, 53
    tahini, 76–77
Middle Eastern specialty items, 14
mint, dried
    Dukkah, 218
    Manakeesh with Lamb and
      Yogurt, 87
    Za'atar Spread, 87
mint, fresh
    Beef Hawawshi Sandwiches, 88
    Cucumber and Garlic Yogurt,
      210
    Dehydrated Tomato and Parsley
      Tabbouleh Salad, 131
    Manakeesh with Lamb and
      Yogurt, 87
    Middle Eastern Steak Tartare
      with Lemon Sabayon, 69
    Seared Falafel Burgers, 76–77
    Whipped Feta with Eggplant
      Relish, 56–57
mishmish, apricot, 194
mo'amar rice with mushrooms and
    truffles, 114
mulberry molasses–glazed duck
    with ginger and cherry
    freekah, 140–41
mulukhiyah, spinach and kale,
    with crisped and spiced
    rabbit, 75
mushrooms
    Chanterelle Cream, 165–66
    and rice loaf with chanterelle
      cream, 165–66
    and rice with truffles, 114
mustard, tahini, 62

nuts. See also almonds; cashews;
    macadamia nuts; pine nuts;
    pistachios; walnut sauce

about, 13
sweet and spiced medley, 58

oil, 13
okra, blistered, with green sauce
    and baked cheese, 132–33
olives, cured, sauce, 172
olives, mango-glazed, and sun-dried
    tomatoes, 54
Om Ali sourdough bread pudding
    with coconut sauce, 183
onions
    caramelized, 156
    and roasted potatoes with
      peppers, 117
onions, pearl
    Braised Beef Cheek Bil Basal, 151
onions, red
    Braised Rainbow Chard with
      Taro Chips, 127
    Chunky Egyptian Tomato
      Sauce, 223
    ful breakfast, 22
    Grilled Calamari with Tomato
      Jam, 171
    Heirloom Tomato Fattoush
      Salad, 105
    Manakeesh with Lamb and
      Yogurt, 87
    Summer Green Bean Fasolia, 106
    Whipped Feta with Eggplant
      Relish, 56–57
orange blossom water, and straw-
    berry compote, 48–49
orange juice: Seared Halloumi and
    Orange-Glazed Beet Salad,
    118
orange peppers: Three Pepper
    Baladi Salad, 110
orange(s)
    rice pudding with fall spices, 29
    and spice olive oil cake, 25
    syrup, 193
orzo and lamb shoulder fattah, 159

pancakes, stuffed Arabic, with
    maple-glazed apples, 189–90
parsley
    hot butter, 155

Kohlrabi and Pomegranate
Salad, 148
sauce, 105
Seared Falafel Burgers, 76–77
Three Pepper Baladi Salad, 110
and tomato tabbouleh salad, 131
passata
Lamb Shoulder Fattah with
Orzo and Crisped Pita, 159
Lentil Ragù, 156
Spiced Rice and Yellow
Zucchini Mahshi, 109
Tomato Béchamel, 124–25
pasta: Macarona Béchamel with
Veal Ragù, 167–68
peas: Seared Falafel Burgers, 76–77
peppercorns: Reverse-Seared Rib
Eye with Dakka, 160
peppers: Three Pepper Baladi
Salad, 110
phyllo dough
cheese squares, 46
Classic Konafa with Wine and
Cherry Compote, 180–81
pickled turnips
Seared Falafel Burgers, 76–77
Yogurt-Braised Shortrib
Shawarma, 83
pies, savoury: Beef Sambousek,
94–96
pine nuts
Beef Sambousek, 94–96
Sweet and Spiced Nut Medley,
58
pistachios
butter, 221
Sweet and Spiced Nut Medley,
58
pita(s)
chips, 105
crisped, 159
Yogurt-Braised Shortrib
Shawarma, 83
pomegranate molasses
barbecue sauce, 144
and kohlrabi salad, 148
potatoes
roasted, with onions and
peppers, 117

salad, with lentils and labneh, 122
powdered sugar
Glazed Orange and Spice Olive
Oil Cake, 25
Kahk Cookies, 197

quince jam, 33
quinoa: Three Pepper Baladi Salad,
110

rabbit, spinach, and kale mulukhiyah, 75
radishes: Heirloom Tomato
Fattoush Salad, 105
ras el hanout
about, 11
homemade, 215
Roasted Cod Sayadieh with
Couscous and Pan Sauce,
152
Sweet and Spiced Nut Medley,
58
red pepper
and roasted potatoes with
onions, 117
Three Pepper Baladi Salad, 110
relish, green pepper, 92
rice
Egyptian, 212–13
and mushroom loaf with
chanterelle cream, 165–66
with mushrooms and truffles,
114
pudding with fall spices and
orange, 29
spiced, and braised lamb with
grape leaves, 66–67
spiced, and yellow zucchini
mahshi, 109
Spinach and Kale Mulukhiyah
with Crisped and Spiced
Rabbit, 75
ricotta cheese: cheese squares, 46
romaine lettuce
Heirloom Tomato Fattoush
Salad, 105
Seared Falafel Burgers, 76–77
rosewater whipped cream, 220
rub, coffee and coriander, 144

saffron butter, 212
salads
dehydrated tomato and parsley
tabbouleh, 131
fingerling potato, with lentils
and labneh, 122
halloumi and orange-glazed
beet, 118
kohlrabi and pomegranate, 148
three pepper baladi, 110
tomato fattoush, 105
sandwiches
basturma, "shortcut," 101
beef hawawshi, 88
fried shrimp, 80
sauces
béchamel, 167–68
black tahini, 134
coconut, 183
cured olive, 172
dakka, 215
green, 132–33
lemon sabayon, 69
pan, 152
parsley, 105
pomegranate barbecue, 144
tahini, 210
tomato, chunky Egyptian, 223
tomato béchamel, 124–25
walnut, 162–63
white, 121
sayadieh, roasted cod, with
couscous and pan sauce, 152
scallions, charred, and grilled
whole fish, 143
seafood. See shrimp
seeds, about, 13
semolina flour
Brown Butter and Coconut
Basbousa, 193
Stuffed Arabic Pancakes with
Maple-Glazed Apples,
189–90
tart crust for Strawberry Pasta
Flora, 198–99
sesame seeds: Dukkah, 218
shakshuka, 26
sharkaseya, chicken, with walnut
sauce and crackling, 162–63

shawarma, yogurt-braised shortrib, 83
shrimp, fried, sandwiches, 80
smoked paprika
    Beef Hawawshi Sandwiches, 88
    Five-Hour "Shortcut" Basturma, 101
    Spicy Turkey Feteer, 97–98
    Yogurt-Braised Shortrib Shawarma, 83
soups
    chickpea and tomato, 91
    leek khisk with crisped kale and onions, 79
    red lentil, 84
    spinach and kale mulukhiyah with rabbit, 75
spice mix
    for grilled Cornish hens, 146–47
    ras el hanout, 215
    for spinach and kale mulukhiyah, 75
spices, about, 9–11
spinach
    and kale mulukhiyah with rabbit, 75
    wilted, 165–66
squid: Grilled Calamari with Tomato Jam, 171
strawberry
    and orange blossom compote, 48–49
    tart (pasta flora), 198–99
sumac
    about, 11
    chicken wings, baked, with parsley hot butter, 155
    pita chips, 105
    Za'atar Spread, 87
sweet potatoes, fire-roasted, 113
syrups
    apricot and honey, 194
    orange, 193

tahini
    black, 42–43
    black, sauce, 134
    ful breakfast, 22

hummus, with sun-dried tomato and caramelized lemon, 42–43
mayonnaise, 76–77
mustard, 62
Not Too Sweet, Not Too Spicy Halva, 229
Pink and Gold Beet Dip with Pine Nuts, 50
sauce, 210
Triple-Sesame Carrots with Goat Cheese, 134
taro root chips, and braised rainbow chard, 127
tarragon, baba ghanoush, 70
tarts
    pistachio, with cookie crust, wild blueberries, and olive oil, 187–88
    Strawberry Pasta Flora, 198–99
tomatoes, cherry
    calf liver on toast, 92
    and parsley tabbouleh salad, 131
tomatoes, grape
    and chickpea halabissa soup, 91
    Pan Sauce, 152
tomatoes, sun-dried
    and hummus, with caramelized lemon, 42–43
    and mango-glazed olives, 54
tomato(es)
    Egyptian sauce, 223
    fattoush salad, 105
    jam, 171
    red lentil soup, 84
    Seared Falafel Burgers, 76–77
    Spiced Rice and Yellow Zucchini Mahshi, 109
    Summer Green Bean Fasolia, 106
    Whipped Feta with Eggplant Relish, 56–57
    Yogurt-Braised Shortrib Shawarma, 83
toum, Lebanese, 213
truffles, with rice and mushrooms, 114
turkey feteer, spicy, 97–98
turmeric

bites, and crispy cauliflower, 45
fayesh, 34
turnips, vinegar glazed, with dukkah, 128

veal
    chop boftek with kohlrabi and pomegranate salad, 148
    ragù, and macarona béchamel, 167–68
vermicelli: Egyptian Rice, 212–13
vinaigrettes
    basic lemon, 209
    yellow pepper, 143
vinegars, 14

walnut sauce, 162–63
whipping cream
    Rosewater Whipped Cream, 220
    Whipped Feta with Eggplant Relish, 56–57
white beans: Black and White Hummus with Sun-Dried Tomato and Caramelized Lemon, 42–43

yellow pepper(s)
    Three Pepper Baladi Salad, 110
    vinaigrette, 143
yogurt
    cucumber and garlic, 210
    Labneh with Garlic Confit, 217
    and lamb manakeesh, 87
    Leek Khisk with Crisped Kale and Onions, 79
    Pink and Gold Beet Dip with Pine Nuts, 50

za'atar
    about, 11
    spread, 87
    Veal Chop Boftek with Kohlrabi and Pomegranate Salad, 148
zucchini
    mahshi and spiced rice, 109
    stuffed, 109